Garden Glory

Garden Glory

From garden boy to head gardener
at Aynhoe Park

TED HUMPHRIS

Illustrated by B.S.Biro

Collins
8 Grafton Street, London W1X 3LA

First published 1969 by
William Collins Sons & Co. Ltd
London · Glasgow · Sydney
Auckland · Toronto · Johannesburg
This second edition with Introduction and Index
first published 1988
© *Copyright Ted Humphris 1969*
© *Copyright Introduction Ted Humphris 1988*

British Library Cataloguing in Publication
Data available
ISBN 0 00 410446 3

Printed and bound in Great Britain by
Robert Hartnoll (1985) Ltd, Bodm.n,
Cornwall

This book has been set in
Garamond 11 on 12 point

Contents

Foreword to New Edition

Garden Glory, and my subsequent book *Apricot Village*, are the story of my life. I realise how lucky I have been: there is nothing special about me. I was born at the beginning of this century to ordinary working-class parents, and went to the village school when I was four, leaving when I was thirteen. I went to work as Garden Boy at Aynhoe Park in 1915. Very soon I was asked to do tasks that normally the boy would not have been asked or expected to do, but times were not normal – the country was at war. Being asked to carry out these tasks not only added interest to my work but was greatly to my advantage, and by the time the war was over I was more or less in charge of the greenhouses. I was always very grateful for any advice from the head gardener, especially when he told me that any task given to me, even if I did not like it or thought it unnecessary, should be done as quickly and thoroughly as possible.

My first real chance came in February 1928 with the death of my employer, Sir Fairfax Cartwright. The death duties levied on the estate were enormous, especially coming so soon after those for his father. Drastic economies were made in all branches of the estate, including the gardens. The foreman gardener left to take a similar position at Woburn, and the head gardener, then over seventy, decided to retire. I was asked to take his place looking after the greenhouses, kitchen garden and orchard with only one elderly man and a boy to help me. It seemed an impossible task but was a challenge I was prepared to accept, especially as I was given a completely free hand. This was a golden opportunity for me, and now I could grow any plants I wished. I intended to grow more orchids and to raise seedlings from my own saved seeds.

Ten years later, knowing I was more or less self-taught and had never been away to any of the large private gardens which in those days were the best training ground for young gardeners, I asked myself whether I was justified in calling myself a professional gardener. I decided to put my knowledge to the test by showing an orchid plant, which I had been growing for more than ten years, at one of the Royal Horticultural Society's London shows in January 1938. The plant was awarded a Certificate of Cultural Commendation, which encouraged me to try again. I soon gained an Award of Merit for a Hippeastrum, and the Lindley Medal for three plants of the orchid Cattleya Portia. This same orchid was awarded the Silver Lindley Medal ten years later, and in January 1960 I was invited to join Percy Thrower on television's *Garden Club* programme. By this time my name was becoming well known to the general public, resulting in my receiving many letters and also visitors to see my plants, especially the orchids. This was at a time most people thought that growing orchids was the prerogative of the wealthy, and that the plants needed specially constructed houses. I was able to show visitors that anyone with a greenhouse and able to maintain a temperature of 50°F could grow an orchid

Because of all this publicity it is not surprising that I was asked why I didn't write a book, but I was never able to find the time even to try. It was not until the end of December 1962 when, as a result of an accident that led to me being away from work for a month (the first time I had been off work through illness for more than twenty years), I began to think seriously about it. I came to the conclusion that I might be able to write a different kind of gardening book because I was born in a historic village, in an old house that I had been given to understand had played a part in the defence of that village during the Civil War; I had worked in and around the same greenhouses for fifty years, working for four generations of a historic family; I had gained several RHS awards; and over a period of forty years I had grown the largest known orchid plant in the world. I would like to take this opportunity of expressing my gratitude for the help I received from my son John who spent many months correcting and assisting me with my original script.

Garden Glory was first published in May 1969, and received a great deal of publicity. Perhaps one reason why the book became so popular was that it was one of the few books to be written by an ordinary everyday working gardener. After it was published I received a large number of letters, not only from people in this country but also from abroad, and many invitations to talk about the book. I have made many pen-friends, especially in America and Australia, many of whom when visiting this country paid me a visit and gave me the pleasure of showing them around Aynhoe.

Readers might like to know what happened to the orchid Cattleya Portia, a plant which more or less ruled my life as a gardener. It is extremely doubtful but for that orchid I would have been invited to appear on television and so would never have written this book. My ambition to see 1000 blooms on the plant was never realised. Time for me had run out. In 1969 the gardens, including the greenhouses, were sold and after fifty-three years I retired. One of my tasks before handing over my keys was to break up the orchid that had become part of my life into suitable-sized pieces in preparation for the journey to its new home in the West Country, where the last member of the Cartwright family was moving to. It is rather difficult for me to describe my feelings as I helped load Portia into a two-tier cattle truck hired from a local farmer and watched it leave Aynhoe which had been its home for so many years.

Now Aynhoe Park Gardens no longer exist and there is nothing left to remind one that once they were well known to many people throughout the world, though Aynhoe Park House still remains. At least *Garden Glory* (and my other book, *Apricot Village*) may serve as a record of that vanished way of life.

As I write this, at the age of eighty-five, I am not quite so fit as I used to be and my gardening days are over, but I am never bored. I have so many memories.

Ted Humphris
November 1987

Foreword

BY PERCY THROWER A.H.R.H.S., N.D.H.

A GARDENER'S LIFE IS A MOST INTERESTING ONE, or at least I think so. This is particularly true if the the gardener was fortunate enough to begin his training in private service when the private gardens were in their heyday. A gardener in those days started off first of all as an improver, then was a journeyman gardener moving about from garden to garden to further his experience, and of course eventually looked forward to the time when he would be qualified to take first a post of foreman, and then of head gardener. In those days the gardener was expected to provide fruit and vegetables out of season, and exotic flowers the year through. Ted Humphris, who has been a great friend of mine for many years, has had this superb training. He has devoted a lifetime to gardening.

I always think the hallmark of a good gardener is the quality of plants that he can grow in a pot. In the large greenhouses at Aynhoe there was always ample evidence of Ted's ability to do this, and he reared fine specimen plants of almost every kind. His greatest pride and joy was always that of growing good orchids. The specimen cattleyas at Aynhoe had to be seen to be believed, and with these Ted Humphris got a number of awards at the various R.H.S. Shows. His cymbidium orchids were outstanding, too. From time to time Ted joined me in Television Gardening Club, and was able to show to the gardening public the beautiful cattleyas, the large cymbidiums with seventy or more blooms on one plant, as well as many others of the fine specimen plants that he grew.

In this book, which makes fascinating reading, Ted relates the experiences that he has had over his many years in gardening, of the services he has given to horticulture, and what is of greater importance, the joy he himself has got from gardening. Far too many famous gardeners have passed on leaving no record whatsoever of their experiences, and the pleasures they have received from gardening. Would a gardener change his occupation? I am sure he would not.

This book will, I am sure, give pleasure to many thousands who are interested in gardening, and help many of us to recall our interesting and enjoyable experiences during our lifetime in gardening. It has my best wishes for the success which it rightly deserves.

Preface

I HAVE BEEN IN HORTICULTURE FOR FIFTY YEARS. As I cast my mind back over those years which have slipped by so swiftly, I become aware of the knowledge I have acquired almost unwittingly, and the countless experiences which flood back to the memory, recalling the nostalgia of days long since past.

So many of our stately homes and large country estates have disappeared and diminished over the past twenty years, so many of them have been swallowed up inevitably in the relentless march of progress of modern times: we have reached the end of an era. It is the realisation of this fact which prompts me to compile this record, and I invite the reader to share my experiences of these past fifty years, and perhaps pick up a few tips from my accounts covering the very wide field of horticulture which I have encountered through my life's work.

I was born at Aynhoe, Northamptonshire, on the 19th November 1901, the youngest son of a family of eight children. Being a large family it was essential that we should live in a large house, and in fact we lived in the largest and tallest of the cottage-type houses in the village. Built of stone, and with a thatched roof, the house was very ancient. The beams, the staircase and all the doors were constructed of oak. One old oak door was liberally studded with square-headed nails. Some of the old stone mullioned windows, which have an iron bar running down the centre, remain till this day. The house was dominated by a large square chimney, which was more than five feet square, and I recall that as a boy I often stared up at the sky above through this immense chimneypiece from the large open fireplace in the kitchen.

My old scout master, whose father was the estate agent during the latter part of the nineteenth century, informed me that somewhere in this old chimneypiece there was an access to a hidden room, this was probably a priest's hole.

My parents had been told that this old house was originally a monastery, although a number of other theories existed. Some locals maintained that it was a wine house, and others claimed that it was a threshing house where the grain was beaten from the corn. I am of the opinion that the first story is the correct one, and that it was in fact a monastery, for the simple reason that with the unlimited building space around, it would not have been necessary to have built a wine house or a threshing house so high, out of all proportion to other buildings in the vicinity.

This house played an important part in the defence of Aynhoe during the Civil War, for a small mullioned window near the apex of the gable about forty feet from ground level afforded an uninterrupted view of the whole valley below, and the rising ground beyond towards Edge Hill.

Another interesting feature of the house was the earth floor in the cellars. The largest cellar, situated on the north side, had a long narrow mullioned window divided into four sections with an iron bar placed vertically across each section. This window was situated just above outside ground level. The cellar was perfectly dry, and was fairly warm during the winter months, and pleasantly cool during the summer, and it was an ideal play room for my brothers and me. One day whilst playing there we discovered a small hole in the floor, and upon probing it with sticks the surface suddenly caved in, very nearly swallowing us up, revealing a hole about three feet in diameter. We had unearthed an old dry well which was all of fifteen feet in depth. Needless to say my father, upon being told of our discovery, filled in the cavity, using soil from the cellar floor around, an act which we children, being blissfully unaware of the obvious danger, resented very much.

Some years later, a possible explanation for this well came to light. Whilst digging the garden about twenty feet from the rear of the house, my father struck a stone with his spade. When the stone was removed a stone built well was uncovered. Tests were made and the well was found to be over fifty feet deep and with a plentiful supply of pure clear water fed by underground springs. No mention of its presence appeared in the records of local wells, but we recalled the discovery of the dry well in the cellar and we concluded that the inmates of the house had at one time made an abortive attempt to direct the outside water supply into the house, perhaps to ensure a plentiful supply of water in time of siege.

My father, who was a gifted water diviner, was able to trace a strong fast current of water from the well in the garden to another well, sixty feet deep, a hundred yards away, this current passing within three or four feet of the dry well in the cellar.

I have passed this old house where I was born almost every day of my life, during which time I have spent over fifty years in horticulture, working in the same greenhouses for four generations of the same family. It is doubtful if any other living person could make a similar claim, although a great many head gardeners could have done so when I was a boy.

Opposite the house stood the entrance to a narrow alley-way which was flanked on either side by six feet high stone walls, and it was along its winding path that I made my way each day to the village school, and in later years to work. It still bears the name of Skittle Alley derived from a game which has been played over the years by the men of the village in which iron rings forged in the village smithy, which was situated at one end of the alley-way, were used. The object of the game was to throw these rings over an iron stake driven into the ground. Wagering on the out-come of these games flourished amongst the spectators, and although attempts were made to bring the offenders to justice, they were always thwarted by the two look-outs who were posted at either end of the alley.

CHAPTER ONE
Aynhoe Estate

THE VILLAGE OF AYNHOE (NOW ABBREVIATED TO Aynho) is of pre-Norman origin, and appears in the Domesday Book as *Aienho*. The name means the hill of Aega or Aegastan, who founded the village in Anglo-Saxon times. On the green near the church once stood a cross. The base of this cross then stood for many years in the stable yard at the Park House, and was used as a mounting block. It now stands at the entrance to my greenhouses.

The circular shape of the village has been maintained since Norman times, and overlooks many miles of the Cherwell valley, with Edge Hill in the distance joining the Cotswold hills. Three church spires situated in neighbouring villages are plainly visible from several vantage points in the village, and an old rhyme passed down through the generations is still frequently quoted regarding them:

> *Bloxham for length,*
> *Adderbury for strength,*
> *King's Sutton for beauty.*

I

At the time of the Norman conquest Aynhoe belonged to a Saxon thane named Asgar, who was a standard bearer to Edward the Confessor. It passed from the thane to Sir Geoffrey de Mandeville, whose family remained there for several generations. The village subsequently passed into the possession of a number of famous families, namely the Claverings, the Nevilles, the Fitzalans (Earls of Arundel), the Shakerleys, the Traceys and the Marmions. In the latter part of the sixteen century, the house was sold by Shakerley Marmion to Richard Cartwright, who took up residence there in 1616. From that time on Aynhoe remained in the Cartwright family in an unbroken succession until 1954, when Richard Cartwright and his only son Edward were killed in a car accident.

At the outbreak of the Civil War, John Cartwright, who was then Squire of Aynhoe, defended his house against the Kings' troops, but like Banbury Castle which stood nearby it was finally taken, but only after the Royalist forces had incurred heavy casualties. After the battle of Naseby, when the Earl of Northampton had suffered a heavy defeat, the Royalist troops retreated towards Oxford, and on reaching Aynhoe, one of the Compton brothers set fire to the Park House, in the year 1645. After the King's cause had fallen, John Cartwright established a claim for £10,000 to pay for the losses he had sustained. The claim was paid in 1680, this being about ten times as much, when a loaf of good bread cost a penny, than £10,000 is today.

Banbury and the surrounding area was of course a Puritan stronghold at the time, and an old rhyme dating back to the time of the Civil War is still popularly known. This parody ridicules the strict Puritan principles, and the ditty goes:

> *Went I to Banbury Oh Profane one,*
> *Where I saw a Puritane one,*
> *Hanging of his cat on a Monday,*
> *For killing a mouse on a Sunday.*

The old village stocks remain to this day, situated in the centre of the village at the side of the main London Road.

They are surrounded by iron palings surmounted by spikes to prevent them from becoming damaged. It is generally believed in the village that Queen Elizabeth I allowed herself to be placed in these stocks when passing through Aynhoe on her return to London following a visit to Warwick and Kenilworth Castles.

One of the most interesting features of the village is the practice of growing apricot trees on the front walls of the houses, a custom which has survived from feudal times, when the fruit from the trees was paid as part rent to the Lord of the Manor. The trees are particularly beautiful at blossom time, when the masses of blooms blend with the stone walls of the cottages. Until about ten years ago a herd of deer roamed the parkland in the village. This herd, also of feudal origin, was one of the few remaining herds surviving in this country. Deer roamed the parkland many years before the first Cartwright took up residence at Aynhoe. I recall that the size of the herd was kept under control by shooting the surplus each year, usually the bucks. The head gamekeeper armed with a special rifle would select a place in which to hide, and the under keepers would then drive the bucks towards him. He never fired at an animal until he had carefully selected the particular buck he wished to eliminate, and was satisfied he could kill it instantly, a task which sometimes took several hours. I once watched the gamekeeper, perched in an old yew tree, shoot and kill a deer, but I never watched again, as I did not like seeing the animals shot.

Oft times however, when the gamekeepers were not hunting their quarry, and the deer were grazing beneath the trees at the top of the park near the shrubbery, making no sound I would creep from shrub to shrub and lie perfectly still watching these beautiful creatures from a distance of only a few yards. I was always advised not to go into the park during the mating season when the bucks would start to fight amongst themselves. At these times the clash of the animals' antlers echoed across the park and the sound could be heard for miles around. I once saw two of these magnificent beasts with their antlers locked together for almost half an hour, striving for mastery.

On one occasion whilst near the park fence I espied two small ears protruding from the grass beneath a clump of walnut trees. Thinking it was a rabbit I crept towards it, and when a few yards away I pounced, whereupon it was my turn to be startled as a fawn jumped up beneath my outstretched arms and bounced away. It had evidently fallen asleep and been left behind when the rest of the herd had moved on.

One day the head gamekeeper walked past the gardens towards the park carrying his deer rifle under his arm. He did not have his dog with him, and thinking this unusual I enquired of him the reason. He explained that he didn't need his dog as he was about to shoot a buck that had an injured leg. This sounded cruel to me and I told the game-keeper so, whereupon he enlightened me. The animal in question was in fact the leader of the herd, and he explained that as soon as the other bucks became aware that it could not defend itself, they would attack and kill it, therefore it was more humane to shoot it. Unfortunately, during the war years when the army occupied the outskirts of the park the deer became very wild and many of them began to roam through the broken fences into the surrounding countryside, causing damage to crops and danger on the roads especially after dark. It was therefore decided that the herd should be destroyed.

Before the herd was eventually destroyed I made a final plea for the preservation of at least part of the stock, and suggested that an enclosure might be made where perhaps twenty deer might be allowed to continue to roam. Expert advisers, however, considered it very doubtful if even this small herd could be successfully confined, and thus regret-tably the idea was abandoned and the whole herd was des-troyed bringing to an end a tradition that had lasted for centuries.

Lying to the south of the Park House is a Yew Walk, which was planted at the time of the Restoration on a huge mound which was the site of the Cavalier burial ground. This Yew Walk terminates in a semi-circular shape, which is protected by a low wall, erected to prevent the unwary from falling thirty feet into the Park below. In later years a platform was built behind the wall, and clay pigeon competitions were frequently held there. A fine old English Rose Garden still remains, situated close to and on the west side of the house.

This is as pleasant a part of the grounds as it was around the year 1700 when it was originally conceived and planted with varieties which were the ancestors of the present roses.

Roses are beautiful flowers no matter what position they occupy in the garden. However the most suitable position for them is an open spot having a southern exposure which is sheltered from strong westerly winds. Such was the site chosen for the old Rose Garden at Aynhoe. It is sheltered by a large cluster of evergreens and a few forest trees, and is open only to the south. *One is nearer to God in a garden than anywhere else on earth* goes an old saying, and I would invite anyone who might doubt this to walk through these rose gardens on an early summer evening, when the scent from the roses and the nearby herb garden fills the air, and the only sounds are those of the song birds, and a gentle breeze whispering through the leaves of the tall limes which stand nearby.

Adjacent to the Rose Garden was a gravel path lined with evergreens, and to prevent the roots from these shrubs spreading into the Rose Garden, a brick barrier was built to a depth of three feet below ground level. To the south of the Rose Garden there is another gravel path over which there stands a series of arches which form a Rose Walk. Some of the old moss and cabbage roses actually had moss growing in the cracks of the bark before they were finally discarded and replaced by varieties such as George Dickson, Golden Ophelia, General MacArthur, Madame Abel Chateney, and Lady Hillingdon.

In the late autumn, after the trees had been balanced by cutting back the long growths, and re-staked where necessary, the beds were mulched with freshly fallen beech leaves. To prevent these leaves from blowing away, a small hedge consisting of branches of evergreens and box was erected a few inches from the edge of the grass. During spring this temporary hedge and the leaves were cleared away, and then using a small hand fork two to three inches of the top soil were removed, and a liberal dressing of coarse bonemeal was forked in followed by a mulching of well-rotted farm manure. Finally the top soil was replaced. This has two advantages, it prevents the food in the manure from drying out, and the fine tilth of soil on top is easier to hoe when it comes to keeping down the weeds.

One old variety of rose grown at Aynhoe was named Gardenia, and as its name implies it was graced with a delightful scent. The flowers were bright yellow during the early stages, later turning to a cream shade. The petals curved in slightly, very similar in fact to the Gardenia itself. On the arches over the Rose Walk, we grew American Pillar, Dorothy Perkins, Crimson Rambler, and Zéphirine Drouhin, the last named being very sweet scented, and bright silvery pink in colour, and because it was practically thornless, a great favourite for cutting.

Two specimen trees which were frequently admired were Frau Karl Druschki, and Dorothy Perkins. The first named, a pure white variety, had a thick stem, and stood about five feet high. The shoots were pegged down so as to form a dome shape. From a distance, especially during the evening, it was a beautiful sight, and this more than compensated for the fact that it had no scent. The Dorothy Perkins rose, which stood on a bank near the tennis court, was supported by an iron stake which was surmounted by an umbrella shaped frame, four feet in diameter, over which the shoots were trained. This delightful rose was always referred to as my tree because I was informed this variety was introduced on to the market during 1901, the year in which I was born.

Of all the roses grown at Aynhoe, two in particular were favourites of mine. One of these was a climbing Lady Hillingdon which was planted against the end vinery wall, facing west, in 1920. It began to deteriorate during the latter part of the 1950's, and finally died during the severe winter of 1962/3. I have gathered roses from this tree for eight months of the year, often gathering a few buds at Christmas time, when the bronze tinted foliage and the apricot-coloured buds provided a most decorative vase.

My other favourite was a very old rose which grew over the roof of the potting shed. Its scent was exhilarating. The flowers which were golden in colour were perfectly shaped whilst in the bud stage, and when opening out assumed the form of a double wild rose. Its leaves were small, and its stems were practically thornless. We called it Sunshine, and this was probably the name given to it by one of the outside gardeners who in his spare time specialised in budding and grafting roses, finding suitable young wild briars in the hedgerows and woodlands. Many of the old roses were introduced in this way, and were therefore never officially named.

A few roses were cultivated in pots for house decoration, such as Madame Abel Chatenay, Lady Hillingdon and Yellow Marshall Neil, the last two named also being grown under glass on the back wall of the vineries to supply early cut flowers.

The Summer House was unusual in design inasmuch as its opening faced away from the sun. Circular in design and with evergreens at the rear, it was pleasantly cool in the heat of summer. Its position afforded an excellent vantage point for witnessing the sunset, and a perfect way to end the day was to sit in the Summer House and watch the sun sink slowly behind the distant hills. The construction of the Summer House provided an object lesson in how the ordinary things around us can be used artistically. The floor was of pebbles selected from gravel pits on the estate, and had a design in the centre, which was picked out with knuckle joints of deer killed in the park. The pointed roof was thatched with rushes, and was supported by six stout oak posts in their natural state. The ceiling comprised hundreds of small cones set into plaster, with a design to coincide with the floor of the building formed from larger cones. All the cones used were gathered from the various conifers growing on the estate. The walls were constructed of osier shoots, and the inside padded with rushes. The curved seat inside the Summer House was built from mis-shapen oak boughs, and was padded with rushes for comfort.

Unfortunately, the Summer House was destroyed by a falling tree during a particularly severe gale in March 1947. The gale which was the worst in living memory created havoc in the Lime Avenue, uprooting the 80 feet high trees, leaving yawning gaps in the proud ranks of the limes.

Standing on the site of the old Summer House is another link with the past in the form of an ancient Saxon water vessel. It is one of a pair which was unearthed by a local ploughman in a field near the village.

Almost three feet in height, the vessels were used as ornamental vases at the Park House. Unfortunately, during Miss Elizabeth Cartwright's 'coming out' party, one of them was overturned and broken, whereupon I decided to fill the remaining vessel with sand thus ensuring that it did not share a similar fate.

One of the woodlands standing on the outskirts of the village is known as the Pest House. The reason for this unusual name is not generally known; however, I recall in the days of my youth an old gardener telling me that when he was a boy he and his parents lived in an old stone-built house situated in the middle of this wood, and the house was known as the Pest House, deriving its name from Pestilence, the old name for an epidemic (and not garden pests as I once thought). In those days, before Jenner and vaccination, any villager suffering from an infectious disease was expelled to this isolated dwelling until he or she had recovered, in order to prevent the spread of infection in the village. Even when I was young this old house had long since fallen into ruins, and had become a playground for the children, and in 1924 it was finally dismantled, and the stone was used to help build a new village hall.

Of all the many rare and beautiful trees standing in the grounds of Aynhoe Park House perhaps the most unusual is a magnificent *Ginkgo biloba*, which is believed to have been presented to General Cartwright by the Rt. Hon. Charles Greville. The Gingko which is a fine specimen lawn tree is also sometimes known as a Salisburia or the Maidenhair tree. It seems that it was originally named *Ginkgo* by Linnaeus under the mistaken impression that this was its Japanese or Chinese name. At that time, about 1758, the flowers had never been seen, and so he was not sure how it should be classified. In 1787, the botanist Sir T. E. Smith thought that the time had come for a new name to be chosen. I presume that by then the flowers and fruit were well-known and the fact that the tree belonged to a unique and monotypic genus had been established. He suggested that the plant should be named after his friend Richard Anthony Salisbury, F.R.S., F.L.S., one of the founders of the Horticultural Society. However, according to the rules of botanical nomenclature, the original name must be taken as the correct one, so the tree has reverted to *Ginkgo* in most modern works of reference. The tree was grown in England before 1750 by the nurseryman James Gordon. It was propagated rather slowly by means of layering, and so remained rare for a long time. It does not flower until mature, and then male and female flowers are borne on different trees. For a long time all the trees grown in England were male. Male branches are grafted onto female trees to produce seed. It is unknown in the wild, and has survived only in the temple gardens of China and Japan. In these countries the nuts are used for food. The *Ginkgo biloba* is also known as Maidenhair Tree, because the peculiar fan-shaped leaves resemble those of the maidenhair fern. Unlike coniferous trees in general, its attractive dull green foliage is deciduous, assuming a clear yellow tone before falling in the autumn. It makes a fine lawn tree and is valuable for small gardens. It thrives in ordinary garden soil and flourishes in town gardens. To preserve a fine pyramidal form, the tree should be pruned in the autumn.

Another specimen tree was a magnificent cedar, *Cedrus libani*, the Cedar of Lebanon. Apart from its historical and biblical associations no tree ever introduced gives so much charm and distinction to a garden. Cones are not produced until the tree is over forty years old. The first known tree raised from seed in this country was in 1685, in the Botanical Gardens at Chelsea. So far, I have not been able to find out if this was the first act of culture in this country, or where, or by whom, cedars were first introduced. Neither have I been able to find any planting record about the cedars at Aynhoe.

It appears that cedars did not exist in this country before 1664, when Evelyn wrote warmly praising the tree, saying that he himself had received cones and seeds from Lebanon, and knew not why cedars should not thrive in this country. The oldest tree known to exist in England was planted in 1676 at Brethby Park, Derbyshire. There was also a very fine specimen growing in a garden near Cobham, Surrey, being about one hundred and twenty feet high.

The Estate was blessed with a vast number of timber trees of almost every conceivable variety. Their beauty and majesty enhanced the whole district, and apart from their

decorative qualities, the timber was used in many ways
both on the Estate and in the village. Amongst the numerous
species of trees to be found in the grounds and the surrounding coverts and woodlands were oak, beech, hornbeam,
chestnut, elm, walnut, lime, sycamore, ash, larch, hickory,
and wellingtonia, to mention but a few. A fine specimen
of the last named variety remains in a commanding position
at the rear of the Park House.

Wellingtonia, *Sequoiadendron giganteum*, sometimes called
Big Wood of California, is one of the tallest growing trees in
the world, having been known to attain a height of over
three hundred feet, with a trunk of ninety feet in diameter.
Some of these specimens are supposed by competent
authorities to be about four thousand years old. It is perfectly
hardy, but likes a fairly sheltered position and a good deep
soil.

Few forest trees excel the common larch in its quiet
beauty, and the tenderness of the young green foliage in the
spring. Furthermore its exquisite flowers are worthy of
study. Apart from this, it is an important tree economically,
owing to its valuable timber. On the Aynhoe Estate, the
timber of the larch trees was used for re-roofing the cottages.

Elm trees abounded in the district and the timber from
these, together with oak, was used to make pump pieces for
the wells in the village. I can remember there being twenty
such wells, all painstakingly built from local stone, ranging
from thirty to sixty feet deep. The water provided from the
wells was pure and clear, and it was carted daily to replenish
the drinking water supply at the Park House.

My father who was a woodman on the Estate was frequently employed in making the pumps for these wells.
Whenever he was engaged in this work his first and most
important task was to select suitable young trees. Only elm
was used and was taken preferably from the hedgerows,
the wood being much tougher than that from the trees
growing in the woodlands.

My father often walked for miles in search of the ideal
timber and was never satisfied with second best. The elm

he finally selected needed to have a trunk at least ten feet long, twelve to fifteen inches in diameter, and unblemished. When it reached the timber yard it was stripped of its bark for the first two or three feet which were eventually sunk into the mud deposit at the bottom of the well. Above this section a number of one-inch holes were bored right through the centre of the piece to a height of about two feet. The next operation, and one that required a great deal of skill, was to bore a perfectly straight hole down through the centre of the piece until a point just below the horizontal holes was reached. If it were possible to see inside the section, the holes bored through the sides would resemble a series of spokes entering the hub of a wheel. The topmost part of the pump piece was gradually tapered to allow another similar length which had been gouged out to fit on top of it, thus forming a watertight and airtight joint.

This procedure was repeated until the last piece reached a point just below ground level. Onto this was fitted the familiar top section which was usually constructed of oak.

When a pump needed to be replaced it was often found difficult for one man to remove the bottom section unaided, particularly if there was mud or clay at the foot of the well, and on one such occasion my father asked for a volunteer to descend the well with him and assist in dislodging this stubborn bottom section. He was somewhat taken aback when a village youth who had often emphasised his dislike of heights stepped eagerly forward to offer his services. Asked if he had at last overcome his fear of heights, he replied 'No, but I'll go down as high as you like'. Needless to say this remark brought forth roars of laughter from those present, and the unhappy youth was never allowed to forget his unfortunate choice of words.

Whilst on the subject of village pumps, I recall that at the lower end of the village, one of the pumps was equipped with a second spout, which was situated above the normal spout and near the top of the erection, its purpose being to allow the horse-drawn water carts to be filled direct. As boys, one of our favourite pastimes was to insert a piece of rag or similar article into the lower spout, and then retire to a safe distance and wait for some unfortunate person to arrive and use the pump and be drenched by the inevitable deluge from above.

A water ram, which is a type of hydraulic engine, was installed to pump water from adjacent wells into vast tanks on the roof of the Park House, to supply the normal water requirements of the household. The overflow from these tanks was piped into the gardens to be used in the green-houses. Before this supply of water was made available, water had to be pumped by hand from a forty foot well situated in the centre of the garden. My father who was also a water diviner told me that he was able to trace eight different water tracks leading to this well.

The value of rain water in a garden cannot be over-estimated, particularly today, when we have so much chlorine added to the main water supply. Every opportunity should be taken to preserve rain water, and at Aynhoe we have water tanks in each greenhouse constructed to hold as much rain water from the roofs as possible. Also the rain water which runs from the roofs of the sheds and out-buildings is directed along pipes to underground storage tanks. When the supply of water was plentiful and the tanks overflowing, we used it to give the vine and peach borders a good soaking.

In addition to the wells there were three water mills on the Estate, and once again timber from the Estate was used to construct the water wheels which operated these mills. Hornbeam and apple were used for this purpose. One mill, which was fed by water from the trout stream which runs through the Park, was known as an overshoot, which means that the water flowed over the top of the wheel, whilst a second mill situated near Clifton, an adjoining village, was known as an undershoot. The water in this instance operated the wheel from underneath, a far greater volume of water being required to drive this wheel, and this was supplied by the River Cherwell. Both of these mills were operating until a few years ago. The third mill was derelict even when I was a child, and was sited close by Raynes Camp to the east of the village. Raynes is an old Roman Encampment which is surrounded by a circular shaped mound topped with trees. Many relics providing information regarding this Roman settlement have been unearthed from this area, and are still frequently found. Recently full scale excavations have been carried out by Oxford University students at the camp, and their findings are currently exhibited at the Ashmolean Museum at Oxford. Old villagers speak of an underground tunnel which once linked the village with the camp, a distance of approximately two miles. There is in fact a large cavern in the side of a hill at the lower end of the village, and the ground rises gently from this point to the camp.

In 1959 the Estate was broken up, the house being sold to the Mutual Household Association. The only part of the Estate to be retained was a small part of the inner garden where most of the greenhouses were situated and the Grammar House. The Grammar House is interesting as before the Tudors it consisted of the dwellings of two Yeomen. In 1654, John Cartwright founded the Free Grammar School there. It ceased to be a school in 1893, when a scheme known as the Cartwright scholarship was instituted in its place, a sum of money being set aside annually to allow one child from the village, upon passing a competitive examination, to attend the Banbury County School for a period of three years.

CHAPTER TWO

My Boyhood Days

OOKING AROUND AYNHOE TO-DAY, AND RECALL-
ing my boyhood days, I realise not without a little
sadness, that very few of the old families remain. I
have been caught up in the exodus myself, and now live
three miles from my birthplace on the opposite side of the
valley. However I do have an uninterrupted view from my
window of my old village nestling in the side of the hill,
with a panoramic view of miles of beautiful English countryside. My cousin Harry is the sole survivor of the Humphris
clan still residing at Aynhoe, and as he has no son, another
tradition will eventually disappear.

The association of old family names with particular
districts and villages provides a fascinating study, and is
worth a little research. Welsh names appear to be closely
linked with Aynhoe for apart from my own family name
which has Welsh origins, there are still many Williams
residing in the village. The explanation for this is that in the

past, sheep and cattle were driven through the village by farmworkers from the Welsh Hills, on their way to the London markets. A bend in the road near Aynhoe Park House is still sometimes referred to as Drover's Corner. Rumour has it that a few head of the stock, whilst passing through the village, would unaccountably stray from the flock or herd, and mysteriously find its way into the field of a relative from Wales who had taken up residence in the village.

In 1924, the bend in the road became more generally known as Wembley Corner. This name came about as a result of the daily stream of motor coaches which passed through the village *en route* from the North and the Midlands to the Wembley Exhibition.

The Church at Aynhoe is dedicated to St. Michael. It is of 14th-century foundation being built during the reign of Edward III. The Norman style tower still remains, although the original four stone figures have disappeared from their niches. The main body of the church was completely rebuilt in 1723 by Edward Wing, a native of Aynhoe who was initially employed as a mason and a carpenter at the Park House. He became very successful as an architect, and designed several London churches, and from one of these St. Michael's was copied.

My father was a bellringer at the church, and whilst he was there the wooden beams supporting the bells were replaced by more dependable iron frames. At about the same time a Carillon was installed. Throughout the years, right from my early boyhood, I have derived great enjoyment from listening to these chimes, and indeed they have become a part of my life. The tunes are played automatically at three hour intervals, between 9 a.m. and 6 p.m. each day, the large clockwork mechanism having to be wound up once daily. Originally the chimes sounded at 9 p.m. also, but this practice has been discontinued since the outbreak of the Second World War when the bells and chimes were banned completely for the duration, and would have been sounded only in the event of an invasion.

For the musically minded the tunes played on the Carillon are as follows:— Sunday—*We love the place O God;* Monday—*God moves in a mysterious way;* Tuesday—*Life let us cherish;* Wednesday—*At the name of Jesus;* Thursday—*The Bluebells of Scotland;* Friday—*Sweet the moments rich in blessing;* and Saturday—*Home Sweet Home.*

When the chimes sound out, the wheels to which the bells are attached move only a short distance backwards and forwards, the hammers of the Carillon striking the bells between the spokes, but when the bells are being rung by the bell ringers, the bells turn almost a full circle, and therefore it has always been the duty of the Captain of the bell-ringers to ensure that the hammers were pulled back before each session, so that the chimes were penned off. Failure to take this precaution would result in the hammers being smashed.

When I was a lad, in preparation for Christmas the bell-ringers began practising on one evening each week from the beginning of November. One year the first practice took place on November 5th (Guy Fawkes night). It was a seasonable evening for there was a very dense fog prevailing. A gentleman arriving late at Aynhoe station, which like so many country stations is situated over a mile from the village, found no conveyance awaiting him, and so he was obliged to start walking. Being a stranger he became hopelessly lost, but then he heard the church bells sounding out through the blanket of fog, and gradually he made his way towards this welcome sound, eventually arriving at the village where he thankfully made his way to the Cartwright Arms Hotel. Once installed in the hostelry he expressed his gratitude to his unwitting benefactors by inviting the team of bellringers to the Inn to drink his health. Furthermore he invested a sum of money to enable the bellringers to make this an annual event on condition that they tolled the bells on each successive Guy Fawkes night. Thereafter, the sum of 10/- was available to the bellringers of the village on the anniversary of this night, for the purpose of drinking the benevolent gentleman's good health, and in those days when beer cost only 1/- per gallon, 10/- purchased a fair amount of ale.

In the latter part of the 1800's, there were only six bells in the belfry. These were rung by six brothers of the Watts family. Their names were Titus, Thomas, Timothy, William, John and James, which, when said in rhyme, were Tite, Tom, Tim, Will, Jack, Jim. This story was told me by the son of James Joseph Watts, a seventy-four year old retired farmer, and as he has no son, another old Aynhoe family will eventually disappear.

I well remember the Rector as a tall striking figure dressed in dark striped trousers, a black frock coat and a tall silk hat, and every Sunday morning after we had attended Sunday School in the village school, the village boys would march dutifully behind him as he led us to the 11 a.m. morning service at the Church. The Squire occupied a pew just inside the Church entrance, and it was his habit to leave the service at the commencement of the hymn sung immediately prior to the sermon. This was no doubt to avoid being caught up in the rush, for we boys were allowed to leave at the beginning of the Rector's sermon, but unfortunately we always left in a far less orderly manner than we had entered.

One incident involving the Rector remains vividly in my memory. I was walking home one lunch hour with two of the old gardeners when the Rector rode by us on his bicycle. As neither of my companions acknowledged the cleric, I likewise did not feel compelled to do so. After riding on a few yards, the Rector dismounted and called me over to him. Very quietly he said to me 'What would you have done if you had not have been with those men?' I told him I would have touched my cap, and then to my surprise he smiled benevolently and said 'Yes, I know you would. I want you to remember that if you know in your heart that it is right to do a particular thing, then do it, no matter whose company you may be in.' I believe that had the Rector rebuked me sternly or lectured me on good manners, the lesson would not have been driven home, but as it was his advice has proved invaluable to me over the years.

Before 1916, although Good Friday was a paid holiday for the Estate workers, there was one condition which was stringently applied, and this required every employee to attend Morning Service on that day. Failure to do so meant the forfeiture of a day's pay, and to ensure that the condition was complied with, the Estate Agent stationed himself near the church entrance and duly made a note of any defaulters.

Many of the village customs, which served to brighten our lives during my childhood, and which compensated us for our otherwise strict upbringing, have alas been discontinued over the years. I think this is a great pity, for they all added colour to English rural life.

One event to which we eagerly looked forward was the Sunday School treat, which was held annually in the Rectory grounds, and justice was done to a large spread laid out on tables beneath an enormous chestnut tree. This was followed by the Sports and Sunday School prizegiving to which parents were invited, and numerous games and competitions followed in the Rectory grounds. One of these games which never ceased to cause much amusement was an elaborate affair. A giant sized clothes basket borrowed from the Park House Laundry was suspended about a foot from the ground by a pole passed through the handles at either end. Each boy and girl took turns inside the basket and attempted to retrieve coins placed on the ground below. Needless to say it was not long before the contestants were catapulted from the basket in their efforts to reach the prizes.

The May Day celebrations were always a very special event in the schoolchildren's calendar. The boys who were taught practical gardening at school were encouraged to grow flowers for the occasion, and on the last evening in April all the children would take flowers to the school and these were mounted on to a large dome-shaped frame made from iron hoops and covered with moss, which comprised the garland. At 9 a.m. on May Day the children congregated in the school playground, and the procession around the village commenced. The honour of carrying the garland fell to the four boys who had grown the best flowers upon it. They were followed by the May Queen and her Attendant, and the rest of the children singing May songs. A halt was made at the Rectory during the middle of the morning, where buckets of lemonade and heaps of buns awaited the parade. The procession took up most of the day, as the surrounding farms and outlying cottages were each visited in turn. The garland was finally returned to the school at 4 p.m. and a final song was sung in the playground before the participants sat down to another spread which had been prepared in the school. There were all kinds of tempting morsels on the tables, paid for by the monies collected by the children during the day.

The Annual Flower Show which was held in the Park grounds was a day in which the whole village joined in. Not only were the men folk able to display their skill in growing flowers, fruit and vegetables, but there were many opportunities for the ladies to demonstrate their abilities. One of the classes in the Ladies Section was for a cooked dinner suitable for a working man, the cost of which was not to exceed 6d., and another was for a cake, the ingredients for which were not to cost in excess of 1/-.

Children were also encouraged to exhibit, and there were several classes open to them, but mainly for them it was a holiday. A ramp was constructed over the boundary wall leading to the parkland below where there were round-a-bouts, swings and side-shows. As night-time descended the grounds were transformed into fairyland by hundreds of coloured lamps. These were in fact no more than painted jam jars with burning candles inside them. Dancing on the lawn to a silver band added to the carnival air of the festivities which carried on till near midnight.

Another great attraction for us was when the foxhounds met in front of the Park House. After the huntsmen, resplendent in their scarlet coats, had partaken of the traditional stirrup cup and the hounds began to move off, we followed them hot-foot vying with each other to open gates in the path of the riders and thus earning a few welcome coppers.

After I started work in the gardens, I was to view the Hunt in a different light. Together with other members of the staff I was posted at a vantage point outside the garden wall in order to turn the fox should it head towards the gardens. Apparently on several previous occasions the fox had sought refuge inside the garden walls and had been pursued by the hounds with disastrous results from the head gardener's viewpoint. I remember that on one occasion the hounds lost interest in their natural quarry, and began to chase after the deer in the park. Although none of the animals was killed or injured, the Squire became very angry at this turn of events and the head huntsman, aware of the obvious disadvantages which could result from his wrath, was swift to apologise. The eventual outcome was that thereafter permission was granted to the Hunt for the young hounds, before they were entered into a pack, to be trained in the park where the Whipper-in particularly emphasised upon them that chasing deer was out.

Another opportunity for the lads of the village to earn themselves some pocket money arose at rook shooting time. On these occasions the local farmers used to gather at the Park House to shoot the young rooks which nested in a two mile long belt of trees separating the main road from the park land. The shoot generally commenced about 4 p.m. and there was always a mad rush out of school amongst the boys, each anxious to offer his services to one of the farmers to carry his cartridge satchel and hand him ammunition as and when he required it. This service could earn the lad 1/- or as much as 2/6d, according to the generosity of the farmer concerned. Each farmer's reputation in this respect was well known amongst the boys, and many a free fight would break out amongst them to decide who should carry for the more generous of the gunmen. Those who were unable to make the grade as carriers would collect the shot birds for which task they received ½d. per head. During the break for refreshments on these shoots, which took place outside the game-keeper's lodge, the farmers would hold impromtu competitions amongst their helpers. About a hundred yards distant was a stream, and a 1/- piece was awarded to the boy who could race there and back first and return with the dirtiest face. The exercise would then be repeated and the prize would go to the boy who returned with the cleanest face.

Often when I was a child, lone travelling showmen would arrive unheralded in the village, much to our delight. I remember the barrel organ man accompanied by his inseparable monkey dressed in red jacket and fez. After his master had played his repertoire of tunes the monkey would knock on the cottage doors and collect the contributions in his fez. Often someone would place a button or some other useless object in the hat, but when this happened the animal would immediately extract the offending article and discard it. The monkey had been well trained. Another favourite visitor was a dancing bear which performed on a wooden platform erected on the village green. Musical accompaniment was provided by the animal's owner playing an accordion, or squeeze box as we used to call it.

A more regular attraction for the children was the arrival of the tinker in the village. We would all gather around his covered wagon and listen enthralled as he told us blood curdling tales, while putting a new bottom on a saucepan, or making a new lid for a kettle. His sinister appearance made his tales all the more fearful, and he was undoubtedly responsible for many a child's nightmare in the villages he visited.

Both my grandfather and my father worked for well over fifty years on the Cartwright Estate, and it may well be that their ancestors did also, but there are unfortunately no records to support this claim. My grandfather, William Humphris, resided at the village of King's Sutton, a distance of four miles from Aynhoe. He told me that from the time he was a boy until he retired over fifty years later, he walked to work at Aynhoe on six days of every week, first as an apprentice and later as a skilled sawyer. In those days, work started at 7 a.m. each morning, summer and winter alike, and the working day ended at 5 p.m. even on Saturdays, and then started the long trek home. Often he would have even further to walk, as the Estate encompassed a wide area incorporating several small villages, and when he was required to work at Hinton in the Hedges, a small hamlet, he covered a distance of eight miles from his home before starting work, and more often than not the Estate Agent would be present to greet him and his fellow workers.

On leaving school my father continued in the family tradition, and as a lad he too walked from King's Sutton each day to work on the Aynhoe Estate. My mother, before her marriage, was a cook, also employed by a branch of the Cartwright family resident at Edgecote situated some distance north of Banbury. My father used to tell me that on more than one occasion during his courting days, after having paid a visit to Edgecote, he would leave there on foot at about 3 a.m., walk home to King's Sutton, where he would change into his working clothes, and then walk to Aynhoe to start work at 7 a.m. In the year 1897 my father, who by that time had been married several years, was offered the old house now known as 86 Aynhoe which had become vacant. He was not unnaturally only too pleased to accept, and he lived there until he died in 1947 at the age of seventy-one. For a great many years, the rent for this old house was only 1/3d. per week, and often my father commented that his employers would have saved money if they had given the house to him, as the cost of re-thatching the massive roof every ten years was far in excess of the rent received for the house over the same period. The rents in the village were eventually raised when electricity was installed in the late 1930's, but at the time of his death my father was only paying a few shillings a week in rent.

My birth certificate describes my father's occupation as a sawyer, and in his day a sawyer needed to be exceptionally skilled with the saw to be so called. This skill was required when selecting the large timber trees for felling, bearing in mind the kind of wood required at that particular time for repairs and improvements on the Home Farms, and in the cottages. I can remember watching my father and my uncle contemplating for several minutes before deciding where the tree they had selected should be allowed to fall so as to cause as little damage as possible to other trees and shrubs. Once they had felled their tree, the boughs would be sawn off, and the trunk would then be sawn into suitable lengths before being loaded onto the timber carriage with the help of two estate horses trained to this type of work. I have seen these horses, when the appropriate word of command has been given, stand perfectly still, taking the strain, because a prop or chain has been in danger of slipping, and I can remember on one occasion seeing one of these animals standing with its front hooves planted firmly on the ground, and with its rear legs stretched out behind it supporting a tree which was leaning over in the wrong direction, and remaining there taking the full weight until some iron wedges were put into place to prevent the tree from falling.

The felled tree trunks were transported on the timber carriage to the timber yard situated near the Park House, and as they were required they were taken into a long shed to be sawn up. Let into the floor of the shed was a pit ten feet in depth, and the tree trunks were suspended above the pit on stout poles ready to be sawn into planks. The instrument used for this task was known as a cross cut saw. It was ten feet in length, and the blade was fifteen inches deep at one end tapering to six inches at the opposite end. It was fitted with two strong wooden handles. Before the cutting operation began, a perfectly straight line was marked along the length of the trunk by plucking a taut length of cord which had previously been dipped in white paint. It was then my uncle's task to stand on top of the tree trunk, grasping the saw at the wide end, whilst my father stood in the pit below in control of the other end of the saw, and attached to the handle at his end was a length of rope which enabled another man to assist on the downward stroke. My uncle's chief task was to keep the saw upright and to direct it along the white line. My father once spoke of an occasion when he and his colleagues had been obliged to fell a tree in a part of the wood where it was impossible to manoeuvre the timber carriage to transport the trunk away, and so they had to dig a pit beneath the place where the tree trunk lay, and saw it into lengths on the spot.

In the past, many cruel sports have existed in rural districts in this country, mainly for the purpose of wagers being placed on the outcome, and indeed a few of these still go on in isolated parts of the country. In my youth, Aynhoe was no exception, and I can recall how wire cages were placed near the rat infested sawdust heap in the timber yard, and when a number of vermin had been trapped in the cages, they were released in the pit and a terrier put amongst them, bets being taken on the length of time it would take the dog to kill them. A story I was told by my father connected with this pastime can perhaps be taken with a pinch of salt. Rumour has it that during one of the barrel organ man's visits to the village, he wagered with the men that his monkey would dispose of the rats more quickly than the dog. Thinking they were on to a good thing, the men eagerly accepted the challenge. The dog polished off its quota of vermin in record time, but then to the amazement of the village men, when the monkey took its turn it grabbed a mallet from off one of the saw benches, dropped into the pit, and swiftly accounted for all its adversaries by hitting them sharply on the head one after the other.

I remember well how almost all of the men working on the Estate smoked clay pipes. These pipes which had extra long stems were popular amongst the working men, and could be purchased for 1d. each. One day I watched one of the men discard an old pipe, the bowl having become cracked. He took a new pipe from his waistcoat pocket and deliberately snapped the stem in two. He then filled it with tobacco, and placed it in his mouth upside down before lighting up. I was curious and asked him to explain the ritual. Straightfaced he told me that he broke the stem, because in its original state it got in the way when he was working, and he smoked it bowl downwards to guard against setting fire to his moustache. After some thought I told him that I didn't believe the second part of his story as I had noticed that all the men smoked their pipes upside down, and they had not all got moustaches. He roared with laughter but when his mirth had subsided he told me the real reason. It was a habit adopted partly to keep the tobacco dry when it was raining, and also it prevented the smoke from getting in their eyes whilst they were working. I watched him re-fill his pipe. He took what looked like a length of black rope from his pocket, which he said was twist. He cut off a small piece, shredded it, and then rubbed it between his palms before pushing it slowly into the pipe and lighting it. When it was well ignited he passed it towards me and invited me to sample it, glancing round knowingly at my father and the men who had by then paused from their work and were looking amused. I knew I could not back down in front of them all, and so I took the pipe and smoked it for a short while before handing it back. I did not enjoy it, and I soon began to cough, and inevitably I was very sick. I heard my father say, 'well he had to learn some time'. Looking back however, I consider that episode as a fortunate one, for I have been a non-smoker ever since.

CHAPTER THREE
At the Garden Gate

IT WAS THE CUSTOM IN THIS COUNTRY DURING THE
early part of this century that children who had
reached the age of thirteen years, and had a position
to go to, were permitted to leave school. Otherwise the
school leaving age was fourteen. When I was of thirteen
years, I had achieved an unblemished attendance record
for the foregoing six years, and I had been awarded a silver
medal by the Northamptonshire Education Committee after
the five year period, and a bar to the medal the following
year. It was the practice at that time for a silver watch,
suitably engraved with the recipient's name, to be awarded
to a child who attended school without being absent for a
period of seven years. I had set my heart on qualifying for
one of these watches, and was determined to remain at
school until I was fourteen years of age to fulfil this ambition.
Imagine my disappointment then, when with only six
months to go, I was informed by the headmaster that the

Education Committee had decided to discontinue the award for the duration of the war. Full of resentment I left school that same week and started work in the village as a farmer's boy, earning 6d. a day working from 7 a.m. until 5 p.m. The schoolmaster had tried his hardest to persuade me to remain on at school, believing that I would have been successful in obtaining a scholarship for entry to the Banbury County School. However I was adamant and disregarded his advice, although I did continue to attend evening classes which he conducted on two evenings each week for children under sixteen years, and the tuition received at these sessions proved to be of considerable value.

I was not happy working on the farm, and was beginning to regret my hasty decision, when the old headmaster who had realised my plight, came to my rescue. About a month after I had left school he called at my house one evening and told me that he had arranged an interview for me with the head gardener at Aynhoe Park, Mr. Brown. The interview was successful and so in July 1915 at the age of thirteen years and seven months I arrived at the garden gate, not because I had any particular flair for gardening at that time, but because work in a small village like Aynhoe was very scarce; and therefore, following in the footsteps of my forefathers, I started work for the Cartwright family, not realising that I should devote a lifetime's work to these very gardens.

I was extremely fortunate to be able to work under a head gardener of the old school. Like most of his kind he was very strict, but he had a vast knowledge of all aspects of horticulture, and he excelled in growing fruit and vegetables. Although I had to learn this side of gardening thoroughly, and was later to reap the benefit of this early tuition when I became head gardener on Mr. Brown's retirement, I soon began to find my vocation in the greenhouses, and I grew to love working under glass, growing all kinds of pot plants, and particularly the growing and care of orchids which followed in the ensuing years. These exotic and exciting plants not only became part of my work, but also my hobby.

When I started working in the gardens the garden staff

consisted of Mr. Brown the head gardener, a foreman,
whose special responsibility was the greenhouses, a second
gardener, known as a journeyman, three men in the kitchen
garden, and myself. In addition two men were employed
full time in the pleasure grounds, and they were assisted
from time to time by other employees from the Estate as
and when required.

The Estate itself was practically self supporting, for it
had its own stone, gravel and sand pits which provided
any building materials which were required, even the bricks
were made from clay found on the Estate. The kitchen
garden in which I carried out part of my duties as a boy
comprised an area of two acres and was enclosed by a
brick wall fifteen feet high. Within this wall was an inner
garden, wherein were situated the greenhouses, frames, the
potting-shed, fruit room and the bothy.

A considerable number of my tasks when I started in the
gardens were confined to the greenhouses. These consisted
of six vineries, six peach houses, one being eighty yards in
length, two large plant houses, and two small growing
houses. Also there were a number of frames, some cold and
some heated. The two large vineries were lean-to houses
built against a wall fifteen feet high, behind which were the
mushroom house and store sheds. The vineries were fitted
with a double row of lights in the roof, supported by stout
rafters. The highest row of lights could be operated to
admit air into the house by means of ropes passing through
pulleys. The lights were each fitted with three catches which
we called notches and when I was instructed to put on one
notch of air, I tugged the rope, thus releasing a catch whereupon the light would glide down about six inches on to the
second catch. Half way down the bottom lights were fitted
iron stops, installed to prevent the top lights from crashing
to the ground should a rope chance to break. In fact this did
happen on several occasions, and the iron stops proved
their worth. One day when I was operating one of the lights
a rope snapped, and in addition to incurring a few bruises
I received a ducking as well, being thrown into a water

storage tank immediately behind me. I doubt very much whether similar roofs exist on glasshouses to-day. They certainly had their advantages for the lights could easily be removed thus giving the vines a complete rest. At the same time the lights could be re-painted, a far easier task when they are completely dismantled. However these particular lights were taken away during the 1930's, and replaced by fixed lights fitted with ventilation gear operated by winding handles. The original old lights are still in use to-day, as they have been converted to fit over cold frames. They are now covered with heavy grade polythene in place of the glass, and are therefore light to handle and can easily be stacked away when not in use.

Improvised frames can quickly be made using this kind

of light, when you have young seedlings which need to be protected. Simply dig out an area slightly smaller than the size of the light, to a depth of about 3 inches, moulding up the excavated soil to form a bank on all sides. When the lights are rested on top you are left with a temporary frame with sufficient room beneath for the seedlings to flourish.

The two large plant houses, which were also fitted with wind-up ventilating gear, faced east and west, an ideal position for flowering plants. These houses were built to a plan drawn up by Mr. Brown almost a hundred years ago, and are still in use to-day. In fact I grow my cymbidiums in one of them.

It was the strict practice when I first started at the gardens that the greenhouses should be thoroughly overhauled every three years. This was carried out on a rotation system, the vineries receiving attention one year, the peach houses the following year, and so on. In addition to these overhauls which included re-painting, all the houses were scrubbed out annually and the walls limewashed. It was one of my chores to ensure that there was a plentiful supply of hot water forthcoming from the old iron copper on these occasions. I remember that one year before limewashing the peach house walls I was given the job of packing cotton wool soaked in paraffin into all the cracks and crevices. On inquiring the reason for this precaution I was informed it was to combat the red spider which had been particularly troublesome during the previous year.

For fifty years before I started work in the gardens, the greenhouses were heated throughout by four-inch hot water pipes, the necessary heat being supplied by boilers situated in three separate stoke holes at vantage points in the garden. The coke needed to feed the boilers was delivered to Aynhoe railway station during the summer months, eight truck loads in all, each containing eight tons of coke. To-day the cost of all this fuel would be staggering, but in those days a ton of coke did not cost as much as a hundredweight would now, especially when bought in such large quantities.

One of the stoke holes was particularly dark and damp,

and one job I used to dislike intensely as a boy was that of cleaning up the ashes there, as a colony of frogs had made it their home. At that time, my dislike for them outweighed their undoubted advantages in a garden.

My first impression of Mr. Brown was of a tall stern looking man, upright in stature, who sported a neatly trimmed goatee beard and a moustache. He always wore a dark suit and bowler hat, and a stiff white wing collar. I cannot recall ever seeing him without this collar, even in mid summer. He wore black leather boots, and one of my tasks was to clean and polish his spare pair each day. So often did I carry out this chore that I can see the tin containing the cleaning substance now—it read *Gishurstine. For protection of boots from wet. Price 6d.* I soon grew to respect Mr. Brown, and indeed I looked upon him almost as a second father. Beneath that stern exterior was a very wise and understanding man. He was a patient man and would always find time to explain his theories to those ready to listen. I certainly learnt a great deal from him, and the knowledge he imparted was to prove invaluable to me during the years to come.

CHAPTER FOUR

The Bottom of the Ladder

THE HOURS I WAS REQUIRED TO WORK IN THE
gardens, appear, when compared with modern standards, to be outrageous. They were in fact from 6 a.m.
until 6 p.m., except on Saturdays when I was permitted to
finish early at 4 p.m.! Wages were 6/- per week, Sunday of
course being a day of rest. These long hours of employment
were not considered as unusual or too arduous by anyone,
least of all by myself, for after all, I was entering into a new
adventure, the intriguing world of the grown-ups.

During the early months in my new world, I was indeed
the garden boy, in every respect, and I was at the beck and
call of all around me, attending to their various needs. One
of my tasks during this time was to lead the pony which was
used to haul the giant mowers across the spacious lawns in
the pleasure grounds. The pony was provided with leather
boots to wear over its hooves, to prevent them from
damaging the surface of the lawn, and it was my responsibil-

34

ity to ensure that these boots were regularly cleaned and oiled.

On one occasion our pony became lame and had to be rested, and for a short period I was obliged to borrow a replacement from one of the local farmers. Unfortunately the substitute pony's hooves were too large for the leather boots, but as the ground was dry we decided to take a chance on carrying out the mowing with the pony wearing no protection on its feet. No difficulties were encountered on the straight, but we soon discovered that its shoes were cutting deeply into the turf on the turns. After some discussion we decided to call in the village blacksmith to remove the pony's shoes temporarily until the mowing was completed. Happily, when this was done we found that the old leather boots now fitted the animal quite comfortably, and the mowing was carried out without any further damage to the lawns.

Once during the mowing, the Green's machine that we used broke down, and after a search in the outbuildings we located its predecessor, a cumbersome piece of machinery which had a cutting area of thirty-six inches; and I recall that when using this monster, I found it necessary to spur the pony into a trot when approaching the turns, to enable the gardener to propel the massive mower round into the opposite direction. It was fitted with a large box which when full contained about two barrowloads of mowings. It was fixed to the machine, and therefore when it needed to be emptied, the pony had to pull the machine to the place of disposal, where the box was winched up by means of a winding mechanism attached to one of the guiding handles until it was above a space situated between the handles, whereupon the box tipped up and the contents were deposited.

By using the pony mower we were able to complete the mowing in half the time it would take two men with ordinary machines. There were of course certain places such as the Rose Garden where the pony could not be used, and these smaller areas were cut with ten or twelve-inch mowers, and some parts with scythes. There was an old gardener who could mow a lawn with his scythe almost as smoothly as it could be done with a lawn mower. Admiring his handiwork one day, watching his scythe gliding effortlessly through the grass, I asked him if he could teach me the art. He showed me how to hold the scythe correctly but he impressed upon me that unless I could learn the secret of sharpening the scythe properly, I would never be able to mow smoothly, without leaving any ridges. My efforts with the scythe were not very successful, and I enquired of the old gardener how he had been taught. He told me with a wry smile that he had learnt the hard way. Whilst still a boy he had been sent into the harvest fields together with two men to reap a field of corn. One of the men went in front to set the pace, and he had followed on behind. The third man brought up the rear wielding his scythe remorselessly right on his heels, urging the unfortunate youngster on when he showed signs of tiring, calling out 'Keep going boy, or I'll cut your bloody legs off.'

It is interesting to note that the first pony mower was invented by one William Budding about the year 1835. The first hand machine was introduced at the 1851 Exhibition, and was made by Alexander Shanks of Arbroath, which is supposed to be one of the many origins of that old saying 'Shank's Pony' when people refer to walking anywhere.

I was very much attached to the little pony. Even during my school days we had become great friends. My father had made a small four-wheeled truck to contain his tools, and during the school holidays I used to accompany him to the part of the Estate where he was working at that time, and proudly lead the pony with the truck of tools hitched on behind. During the warm sunny days in the summer holidays, whilst my father was at his work, I used to spend very many happy hours roaming the fields with the pony as my companion. He came to me instantly whenever I called his name, but many of the men on the Estate who did not have such a close understanding with the animal could be heard calling it many other names besides its own whilst attempting in vain to catch it to begin the day's work at 6 a.m. in the morning. After I started work in the gardens, I often used to steal away to the paddock where the pony was kept and take him an apple or a carrot, and on mowing days I always managed to scrounge a few handfuls of corn from the head groom to add a little flavour to the pony's midday meal.

An amusing incident which occurred on a neighbouring estate in those days is worth relating. The mower on this estate was drawn by a donkey named Jack, and apparently whenever the large lawns in front of the Mansion were being mown, the butler was in the habit of taking a pet parrot on its stand out on to the terrace for some fresh air. The parrot, having no doubt been well briefed by the butler, called out 'Whoa Jack' whenever the donkey came within ear-shot. Needless to say the donkey needed no second bidding when being told to stop, and although the boy leading the donkey found the exercise amusing, one can imagine the annoyance of the gardener who was trying to get on with the mowing. It seems that things eventually came to a head when one day the gardener had halted the mower to carry out some running repairs, and was applying his spanner to the offending nut when the parrot un-accountably reversed his routine and called out 'Gee up Jack', whereupon Jack immediately obeyed, and as the mower started forward the spanner catapulted from the gardener's hand cutting his forehead and dislodging his cap in the process. This was the last straw for the hapless gardener, who there and then stormed into the house, and told the butler that if he didn't remove his parrot at once he could do the mowing himself in future. The butler must have thought that the gardener meant business for the parrot was never seen on the terrace again on mowing days.

Each Tuesday, I was detailed to assist in the Laundry at the Park House. My particular task was to turn the handle on the mangle. This was no ordinary mangle, and although the mechanics of this awesome machine defy description, I will endeavour to explain how it operated. Four large wooden rollers rested between two wooden blocks. The bottom block which was a fixture was slightly longer than the one above. The top block of wood resting on the rollers was propelled forward when the handle was turned, and in so doing the rollers were rotated. Throughout the operation, the leading roller, on reaching the end of the press, was removed, and a replacement roller was inserted at the rear of the press. Simple though my menial task might appear, I had to take particular care that I did not turn the handle too fast, because not only did this mean that the linen was not properly pressed, but the leading roller, having reached the end of its journey, would crash to the floor. I soon learnt to operate the mangle most carefully, for when the laundry was completed to the satisfaction of the head laundry maid, and she considered that I had performed my task well, she would send to the kitchen for a pot of tea and a plate of fancy cakes as my reward.

The remainder of my working week was taken up by numerous duties, such as weeding, scrubbing the staging and floors in the greenhouses, running errands and making myself useful to the foreman gardener, who resided at the gardens, in the bothy.

Another of my tasks at this time was to prepare the wood and coal, and light the fire in the bothy. This done I was then required to lay the breakfast table for the foreman gardener. Whilst doing this one morning, I caught sight of a phonogram standing on a side table, with a record already on the turntable. Unable to resist the temptation, I set the mechanism in motion, and played the record through very softly so that it should not be overheard. That evening when the hour to go home was approaching I was summoned to the bothy, where the foreman wished to see me. This was not unusual as I was often required to call in at the bothy before going home to collect the letters for posting. I knocked at the door, and the foreman bade me enter. He guided me into a room, where there was a cup of tea, some bread and butter and a piece of cake on a table. He informed me that this was my tea. Naturally I was puzzled, until he drew my attention to another table on which rested the phonogram, and beside it an enormous pile of records. 'Now play the bloody thing, and perhaps that will teach you not to touch anything in future, without asking permission' stormed the foreman as he left the room. Well do I recall that I spent the next two hours playing the pile of records at the fastest speed possible, and only after the whole repertoire had been exhausted was I allowed to go home. It was a lesson I never forgot.

One of the jobs which was allocated to me, and one which I always found tedious and boring, was that of sponging down the large palm trees. I was thus engaged one winter afternoon, when due partly to the heat of the greenhouse in which these tropical plants were kept, and partly through lack of interest in what I was doing, I fell asleep. When I awoke, it was dark, the garden doors had been locked and everyone had left. To go to the bothy and enlist the aid of the foreman was more than I dared to do in the circumstances, and so I made my way to the perimeter wall which I scaled by climbing one of the pear trees which were horizontally trained along the inner wall.

I had very little to do with the head gardener, who in those days was always addressed as 'Sir', and in fact one was not permitted to speak to him unless he spoke first.

When I was sixteen years of age, Mr. Brown engaged a man in the gardens, who had been invalided from the army with war wounds. Although this man did not intend to make gardening his permanent career, he excelled in growing pot plants. He specialised in growing particular species for short times. For instance, one year he concentrated on calceolarias, and then as winter approached he switched to zonal pelargoniums. I recall he staged a group of the latter in one of the vineries which was the finest display of its kind I have ever seen. Unaccountably, he would lose interest in the plants he had raised and would concentrate on something entirely different. When this happened he handed his charges over to my care, and I eagerly grasped the opportunity, and accepted the challenge gratefully. I concentrated on remembering every little thing he had done in growing the plants, and I was determined that I would grow the plants as well as he had, even returning to the greenhouses in the evenings after work in my own time to care for the plants.

The ex-soldier was housed in the bothy, and shortly after he moved in I was invited to join him. I realised that this would be a great help to me, especially as I had resolved by that time to make gardening my career, and so I accepted the invitation and went to live within the very garden walls in which I was working.

The bothy is the name given to a house or rooms in which the single gardeners on an estate reside, particularly those working in the greenhouses. Usually they consisted of rooms situated above the potting shed, store shed, or stoke hole. At Aynhoe we were more fortunate, as Mr. Brown had been able to persuade the old Squire to build a new bothy during the end of the last century.

The new bothy was in fact a fairly modern bungalow with spacious rooms and separate bedrooms. It was furnished from the servants' quarters at the Park House, and in fact residents of the bothy were recognised as indoor staff, and as such were invited to such functions as the Servants' Ball. A woman, usually the wife of one of the outdoor gardeners, was employed to do the housework and cook our midday meals, except on Sundays of course when we had to fend for ourselves. Each Saturday morning I drew any cleaning materials which we needed from Mr. Brown, who once a month, accompanied by Mrs. Brown, visited the bothy and inspected the linen. We were allowed a supply of free fruit and vegetables, and milk from the Home Farm, and by keeping on the right side of the keeper, a couple of rabbits or a joint of venison would sometimes come our way, and this would help to keep the meat bill low. This all meant that we only needed to purchase a few items from the village shop. I used to keep the accounts for the two of us, and at the end of each fortnight when we received our pay we paid off our accounts which amounted to about 11/- each.

A good bothy was always considered to be a great asset, and the availability of such a dwelling appeared prominently in the 'Situations' columns in the *Gardener's Chronicle*. Over forty years ago, I remember in this publication a head gardener advertising for a first journeyman concluded his advertisement with the words 'No long-haired poet need apply'. The term journeyman applied to those gardeners between the positions of foreman and garden boy. In some of the larger establishments there was often a 1st, 2nd, 3rd, or even 4th, journeyman in each department.

My wages at the age of sixteen years were 12/- per week plus an additional 5/- on alternate weeks for duty, which meant that from midday on a Saturday until the same time the following week, you were responsible for the gardens, particularly the greenhouses, and furthermore you were not allowed to leave the gardens during your week-long tour of duty. At any time you might be required at the Park House for some chore, and the head gardener expected to find you either in the gardens or in the bothy at any hour of the day and night during your tour of duty. Often I was called out to start up fires in the stoke holes when it was found that the temperature in the greenhouses had become too low. It was impossible to shirk one's responsibilities in this respect, for each evening either the head gardener or the foreman set the small indicating needles on the thermometers which registered both the minimum and maximum temperatures reached during the night. Another task allotted to the man on duty was that of unlocking the garden doors in the mornings to admit the outdoor staff, and locking them up again in the evenings as they left. Towards the end of the war years, the stringent conditions imposed upon the duty man were happily relaxed, and the imposition of maintaining an exact unfluctuating temperature in the greenhouses was discontinued, and provided you carried out all your proper duties correctly it was no longer necessary to remain within the garden precincts after normal working hours.

After I had been in the bothy for six months, my companion, a married man, requested that his wife be allowed to reside there with him. His request was granted, and I returned to live with my parents again. However, eighteen months later the man and his family left the village, and I returned to the bothy, and this time I shared the quarters with a very skilled all-round gardener who had arrived at Aynhoe from the gardens of the late Sir Ernest Cassel. About a year later, economies were made on the Estate, and the bothy was closed. A number of the staff also became redundant, and indeed I would have been one of the unfortunate ones if it had not been for the decision made by my companion at the bothy, who was the foreman gardener. He did not take kindly to being ejected from the bothy, and he refused to find lodgings in the village. He therefore found himself a new position, taking over the Glass department at Woburn Abbey, the home of the Duke and Duchess of Bedford. As a result, I was placed in charge of the greenhouses at Anyhoe, and I was allowed a garden boy to assist me. Thus a period of crisis suddenly became for me a moment of great opportunity.

During the months that followed I made a number of visits to Woburn Abbey to see how my old colleague was faring. The bothy in which he resided there was a far more palatial affair than the one at Aynhoe, and the living quarters were situated on one side of a road, whilst the sleeping quarters were situated on the opposite side alongside the potting sheds. At this time they grew every type of fruit imaginable at Woburn, and some of the finest Muscat grapes and melons that I have ever seen, as well as a very wide range of plants. My periodical visits to Woburn afforded me golden opportunities of learning how to grow plants that up until that time I never knew existed, and the knowledge I gained there became extremely beneficial to me when I eventually became head gardener at Aynhoe and was in a position to choose for myself what I wanted to grow.

During these early months at the gardens I frequently came into contact with Richard Cartwright, referred to then by most of the villagers as the Young Squire. He was about eighteen months my junior, and although I was only the garden boy, we spent many happy hours together in the grounds sharing our teenage interests, among which of course was searching for birds' nests. On one occasion the Young Squire brought to the gardens a number of small cacti. We took these plants into one of the greenhouses, and together we constructed a large sand table. The sand represented the desert and we planted the cacti amongst it, and used small arab figures with their camels to give the whole realistic finish. Several years later when we had grown older this little tableau was swept away, but, although I have never been particularly keen on cacti, several of these original plants were salvaged, and some of them remain to-day, and serve to remind me of part of my childhood. The interest in cacti which existed in the gardens at that time arose from Sir Fairfax Cartwright having been at one time a British Attaché in Mexico, where of course the cactus abounds. Having become interested in these fascinating plants, he bought a number of the species home with him to England. As for my own experiments with cacti, in April 1939, and again in June 1951, I exhibited at the Royal Horticultural Society Show a large pan of *Mammillaria elongata*, in flower, and on both occasions I received a Certificate of Cultural Commendation.

A task in which all the outside staff would assist was filling the Ice House. Similar constructions have existed on a number of country estates in this country, and they are of great interest. The Ice House at Aynhoe was built in 1818 and remains to this day. Constructed of brick, it stands in the pleasure grounds quite close to the Park House.

Built in the shape of a large egg, it has a depth of twenty feet and is fifteen feet in diameter. Most of the structure lies beneath the ground, but the soil which was initially excavated was piled on top of the part of the building protruding above the ground, and thus resembled a gigantic molehill. Subsequently this dome-like roof was planted, and became a delightful rockery, and the whole being surrounded by laurel bushes was continually shady and cool. Access to this tomb was by way of a passage built into the east side of the

mound. The passage-way led towards the north side until
a thick oak door was reached. On the other side of the door
was another passage-way, six feet high and five feet wide.
This led to yet another door, and beyond, another small
passage-way. It was a rule that one door had to be closed
before opening another, so as to prevent air infiltrating
from outside.

It could be said that the Ice House was the forerunner of
the refrigerator, and it must have been invaluable to the
village community in its early days. The House would be
filled following a particularly severe spell of weather, when
the canal and ponds in the area became frozen over. The
tenants would provide horses and carts to assist in conveying
the ice to the Ice House, and on arrival, the ice was broken
into convenient sizes and then wheeled in barrows into the
building. As each barrow-load was tipped into the deep
bowels of the Ice House, the ice was levelled and the walls
lined with straw. (This was usually the task of the garden
boy.)

In these conditions the ice would remain in its natural
state for a period of two years, and during this time, when-

ever ice was required in the Park House it was always readily available, and should anyone in the village fall ill, then ice was supplied, provided written authority was obtained from the doctor or village nurse.

The Ice House was also used as a cold store, the carcasses of deer, pheasants and hares being laid on the ice for future use at the Park House. I recall that following a shoot in the Park, my brother was given the job of laying some pheasants on the ice. He made the mistake of laying them around the walls of the structure, for when the ice began to subside it left cavities around the walls, and needless to say the pheasants disappeared. There was consternation when the kitchen staff called to collect the game and found that it had all vanished. But all was well when it was eventually recovered from the depths of the Ice House.

Nowadays, when refrigerators and deep-freeze units are commonplace, few people are aware that in the past, the only way one could have iced drinks in the country houses during summer time was with ice stored in underground ice houses.

Those houses that did not possess permanently built ice houses built temporary ones each year. These were usually dug out of the ground and covered over, or cut into the side of a hill. A large excavation was made and then posts were driven into the earth, about 2 feet from the walls of the excavation. The space between the posts and walls was then lined with insulating material. The ice, packed around with straw, usually lasted through the summer months. The top, if not dug into the side of a hill, was covered with 3 to 4 feet of insulating material and finally topped with a foot or so of soil, in which evergreens were planted.

I wonder how often the old-time gardeners watched the gentry on a hot summer day, sipping their ice cold drinks on the terrace or under the trees on the lawn, and bitterly recalled their numbed fingers as they had cut and stacked the slabs of ice during the previous winter.

In November 1915, William Cornwallis Cartwright, the old Squire, died, and his only son, Sir Fairfax Cartwright, inherited the Estate, and I clearly remember that upon this sad occasion it was my task to gather a large quantity of moss with which to line the grave of the old gentleman. Although it was the usual practice in those days to use wire netting for this purpose, the moss being pushed in between the wire, on this occasion canvas sheets were used, and I spent three days sewing on the moss I had gathered.

I also remember that at the head of the grave we wired white chrysanthemums into the canvas, in the shape of a large cross.

CHAPTER FIVE

Growing Up in the Greenhouses

O N JANUARY 1ST 1916, SIR FAIRFAX AND LADY
Cartwright took possession of the Estate, having already taken up residence in a dwelling in the village,
which was known as the Grammar House. However, although the new Squire had decided that a smaller residence
would be more to his liking, the Park House carried on in
the same manner as before with a slightly reduced staff of
servants, and Sir Fairfax and Lady Cartwright frequently
entertained and accommodated guests there.

The Grammar House is an attractive building, built of
stone, and stands in its own grounds near the main road at
the southern end of the village. An unusual feature of the
house is a sundial built into the front wall just beneath the
roof, which bears the quotation 'Yet a little while is the light
with you. Walk while ye have the light'. John XII (35). It
also bears the date 1671, which is probably the date of
completion, and the letters M.C., being the initials of the
first Cartwright to live there.

The garden at the Grammar House contained six large ornamental vases, similar to those at the Chigi Palace, in Siena. These vases had been brought from Italy as Lady Cartwright was Italian. In Italy, lemon trees were grown in them, but at Aynhoe they were planted with wallflowers and myosotis in autumn, and with orange and lemon African marigolds in summer.

Lady Cartwright was particularly fond of flowers, and derived great pleasure from their presence, and as a result the cultivation of fruit under glass began to take second place. More and more pot plants were required for house decoration, and consequently the vines in one of the vineries were cut out, and soon afterwards a similar fate overtook the adjoining vinery.

One of Lady Cartwright's favourite flowers was the sweet-scented violet. It is believed that this exquisite flower originated in the Moorish gardens of old Spain, but some claim that it came from Turkey via Italy. It was also the favourite of Napoleon, and Josephine wore violets on her wedding day. Thereafter Napoleon gave her a bouquet of fragrant violets to mark their anniversary.

In this modern age it is possible to buy bunches of violets, if one is prepared to pay the price, at almost any time of the year. This however was not possible when I began my gardening career, and if violets were required in winter they were grown in frames.

Violets can be grown in almost any soil or situation, but in order to produce special results good soil and cultivation are necessary. To obtain large flowers in winter one must begin with young healthy plants. To produce these a start is made in the spring by dividing the old plants, using only the strong healthy side growths and planting them in a well cultivated plot. By continually using the hoe, keeping the plants watered and syringed during dry spells, and adding a dusting of old soot, strong healthy plants can be produced for the autumn.

Violets are perfectly hardy, but to produce fine flowers in winter, frames are necessary, and if one has heated frames, the task is easier especially during damp and frosty weather.

At Aynhoe we had no heated frames to spare, so we provided a certain amount of warmth by placing the frames on a mild hot bed in what was called the frame yard.

This area was always a little untidy and so it was surrounded by a six-feet high beech and privet hedge, although it was slightly lower on the south side to allow more light and air into the yard.

Having a large number of beech and oak trees at Aynhoe, we always maintained stacks of leaves some of which were several years old. After the summer months we selected the less decayed leaves, to which we added fresh stable manure thus providing the ingredients for the hot beds. It may seem laughable to-day, but I remember we asked that the manure which the horses had well watered be put aside until we had sufficient for our needs.

The hot bed was made at least two feet larger than the frame, the frames used being eight feet by six feet. The bed was trodden down and then liberally sprinkled with soot as a deterrent against worms, the frame then being placed in position. The frame itself was then three parts filled with a rich compost consisting of three parts finely chopped loam, one part leaf soil rubbed through a half-inch sieve, one part of dried cow manure or compost from a spent mushroom bed plus a liberal sprinkling of coarse bone-meal and old soot, the latter being mixed in separately, together with some crushed mortar rubble and coarse silver sand to keep the compost porous. The bed was then lightly trodden down and thoroughly watered.

As soon as the frame bed had dried out sufficiently, strong healthy plants were transferred into it from the outside border and planted, leaving a space of six inches between each plant, and three to four inches from the glass of the light when placed on the frame. This spacing is important because to ensure that the plants remain healthy, air must be able to circulate freely amongst them, and there must be plenty of room for the surface soil to be lightly forked over at frequent intervals.

Immediately after planting, the lights were replaced on the frames until the plants had become established in their new quarters, after which they were removed until the nights began to get colder, and then they would be put back on at night propped up by a brick. The lights were frequently washed to allow maximum light to reach the plants.

With the approach of winter a mixture of leaves and fresh stable manure was packed round the frame until only the lights were visible. These were covered at night time with plaited mats whenever frost threatened.

The chief enemy during winter was not the cold, but the damp weather, and to help keep the surface dry and to absorb some of the moisture, the surface of the bed was covered with a thin layer of granulated charcoal. Whenever the plants required water the charcoal would be collected up and the soil between the plants was watered, using a small can. Care was taken to ensure that no water came into contact with the crown of the plants, nor as far as possible the outer leaves. Before nightfall the charcoal was replaced, but even with all these precautions some leaves and leaf stalks would damp off and need to be removed otherwise decay crept into the crown of the plant.

Removing these decaying leaves, and pinching back the side growths was a tedious and back-aching job. Back-aching because one was not allowed to step into the frame, and as the frame was completely buried, it was necessary to kneel on a board placed across its top.

One day over fifty years ago, although I remember it as if it was only yesterday, I was so employed and feeling terribly bored when suddenly a voice behind me said 'Boy, you don't like that job'. Turning round on the board I saw Mr. Brown and for a few seconds I did not know what to say, because I knew I had not been paying proper attention to my work, and I was a little anxious because I knew that on the slightest instant I could be dismissed, as there were plenty of other lads in the village who would eagerly have taken my place. I owned up and said 'No Sir'.

Much to my relief Mr. Brown said 'No, neither did I when

I was a boy so I will give you the same advice that was given to me. If you have a job to do, one you do not like, do it as well as you can, and as quick as you can, and at the same time think about the time when you yourself can tell someone else to do that self-same job.' I have often thought of those words although I have never found it necessary to ask anyone to do that particular job under those circumstances, because as the years passed I had thought of an easier way of growing violets in pots.

Initially I use the same method, but instead of putting compost in the frames, I half fill them with sifted leaf-soil, then decide how many plants are required to fill the frames, and wash the necessary six-inch pots. I recall how often I was told about thoroughly washing pots, sometimes being made to wash them a second time. Countless times it was impressed upon me that a dirty pot would not allow air and moisture to pass through, also the old soil clinging to the sides of a dirty pot often contains disease spores; and finally how difficult it could be when removing a plant from a dirty pot not to damage the roots. The foreman made me learn these rules off by heart and repeat them to him. The compost I prepared was made up of four parts of good turfy loam finely chopped, one part of leaf mould, one part of well rotted manure, or manure from an old spent mushroom bed, and to each bushel of compost I added a six-inch pot of coarse sand and a four-inch pot of old dry soot all thoroughly mixed together.

It was while lifting a particularly fine healthy plant that I noticed particles of bones clinging to the roots, probably a hen or rabbit had been buried nearby. This made me realise that it might be possible to raise even healthier violet plants by adding a liberal supply of phosphates in the form of bones, and so instead of using crocks for drainage purposes in the bottom of the pot I substituted crushed bones.

After the plants have been potted they should be well watered, allowed to drain, and then sunk to the level of the rim of the pot into the leaf soil inside the frame. The same care is needed as regards airing, watering and matting up at night. The real advantage is that by growing in pots it is a simple matter to lift out a pot and remove the decaying leaves, and water the plant when necessary and return it to the frame. Furthermore when space becomes available in the cool greenhouse plants can be taken inside.

During my early days in the gardens I was told the names of the plants with which we had been working, and encouraged to ask questions and to seek information and advice from books about them. This was so with the violets.

At Aynhoe we grew three varieties of violet, namely Prince of Wales, which had blooms more like a viola than a violet with single dark blue flowers, the stalks of which were from six to eight inches long with an erect habit, and having great vigour; the double Parma violet Marie Louise, which was the most popular one, not so vigorous as Prince of Wales with rich lavender blue flowers with a white eye; and a third called Neapolitan with lavender coloured flowers with a white eye, abundant and very fragrant.

We also provided plants for the Christmas, Easter, Whitsun and Harvest Festivals at the Church, undertaking to supply two groups of plants arranged on either side of the altar. Each group consisted of a palm and three pots of arum lilies for the Easter and Whitsun Festivals and a palm and three pots of white chrysanthemums for the Harvest Festival and Christmas; the pots themselves were camouflaged by specially trained plants of the silver variagated euonymus. In addition there were placed around the font and the lectern well-grown plants of stocks or cyclamen. This sequence of decorating had remained unchanged since the middle of the 1800's.

The glass house which was heated to the highest temperature we called the Stove House, and in it we cultivated palms, gardenias, dracaenas, caladiums, crotons, and many varieties of fern. Also trained along the trellis-work suspended from the roof were stephanotis and bougainvillea.

Stephanotis, or as it is sometimes called the Clustered Wax Flower, grows extremely fragrant small white flowers. It requires a warm temperature, and should be trained on pillars or along trellis-work. It should be watered freely during its growing period, and should be pruned during early spring, when all strong growth should be cut back and weak growth removed. It is important to shade this plant from strong sun.

Bougainvillea is a deciduous stove climbing plant, and is particularly suited to a trellis screen at the rear of a lean-to greenhouse. Its chief attraction is the wonderful loose panicles of richly coloured leaf bracts, which have in their centre small white flowers similar to a hydrangea. John Innes Compost No. 2 is ideal for this plant, which should also be watered freely during the growing period. Watering should be reduced after it has flowered, and during the winter months it requires very little water at all. The previous year's growth should be pruned to one inch of the base annually, as the flowers are born on the current year's wood. All weak growth should be cut away.

Another climbing plant in our collection, and one which can be grown in a cooler greenhouse, was *Lapageria rosea*, named after the first wife of Napoleon, whose maiden name was Marie Josephe Rose Tascher de la Pagerie, and whose first husband Alexandre de Beauharnais was guillotined in 1794. She was born in Martinique. Discovered early in the 19th century in Chile, this plant is sometimes known as the Chilean Bellflower. Its green leathery leaves and its rich crimson flowers make it one of the most beautiful of all climbing plants. At Aynhoe, we trained the plants along canes, for we found that the lapageria resented wires. Compost consisted of peat, fibrous loam, sand and clinkers, the last ingredient being used for drainage. Also in its favour is its ability to flourish even outside a greenhouse, when a suitable shady spot can be found.

Amongst other plants grown under glass at Aynhoe were begonias (especially the Lorraine strains), gloxinias, cyclamen, cinerarias, fuchsia, camellia, oleander and datura.

The fuchsia were trained along wires suspended from the roof of the greenhouse in a similar manner to vines, being pruned in the same way. When in bloom they made a glorious sight, and indeed fuchsia can be best appreciated when looking up into the blooms.

The camellia of course is the favourite of many, and therefore deserves special mention. A moist atmosphere is essential for this plant, as dryness will cause both the leaves and buds to drop. It should be watered freely during the growing season, but from September onwards it is sufficient to water enough to prevent the compost from drying out. A top dressing of peat or leaf soil is beneficial, and when pruning one should bear in mind the general shape of the plant. At Aynhoe, we possessed a fine specimen, which had been trained over the years so that it resembled a large ball. It was planted in a large tub, and its double red blooms always appeared in December, and were used for decoration on the inner table at the Park House on Christmas Day. The flowers were taken from the plant by giving them a sharp twist, preventing damage to the growing shoots. They were then wired into a bed of holly to complete the decoration.

Oleander, or Rose Bay, is another lovely greenhouse flowering shrub, the flowers of which have a wonderful fragrance all of their own. It is a native of southern Europe, and records show that it was popular as long ago as 1596. It is reported to be poisonous, as indeed is *Datura suaveolens*, a greenhouse shrub which bears large white blooms, sometimes referred to as Angels' Trumpets.

CHAPTER SIX

Vegetables

ALTHOUGH THE GLAMOUR OF THE GREENHOUSES inevitably imprints itself on my mind, the main part of the gardens was devoted to vegetables, which provided the House with a variety of produce all the year round. I will mention some of the most popular and outline a few hints which may prove to be useful to those who grow their own vegetables in their gardens or on their allotment.

We grew thirteen beds of asparagus each twenty-two yards long and five feet wide, some of which were over fifty years old. I remember that one of the first sights which met me when I first started work at the gardens was this large area of asparagus fern which was taller than I was. The fern was allowed to grow until the autumn, when it began to turn yellow. The ferns were then cut down to three inches above ground level with a sharp scythe. After the beds had been cleared of the stems and weeds, the surface soil was raked off into the pathways between the beds, leaving many of the roots exposed. A dressing of three to four inches of well-decayed manure was then applied to all the beds, after which the soil previously raked off was shovelled back leaving the beds neat and tidy for the winter. We always took the precaution of using manure from the centre of the heap, thus ensuring that the majority of weed seeds were destroyed by the heat given off; failure to take this precaution meant a tedious job of weeding, possibly by hand, in the spring. In February and again in early April a liberal dressing of agricultural salt was sprinkled over the beds, this also helped to keep the weeds in check.

Cutting usually started during April, the shoots being cut about three inches below ground level with the aid of a special knife fitted with a long blade with a saw-like edge. It is common practice to stop cutting asparagus towards the end of June, to allow the remaining shoots to grow and thus strengthen the crowns for the following year. At Aynhoe we curtailed the cutting during the first week in June, and thereafter we restricted the cutting to shoots growing close together ensuring that sufficient shoots remained to fill the beds, and by employing this method, we were able to cut the odd bunch of asparagus right into July, by which time the remaining shoots had reached a height of two to three feet.

Whenever a crown ceased to produce shoots or it showed signs of exhaustion by only producing very thin shoots it was dug out and replanted. To ensure a regular supply of fresh stock a row of asparagus was raised biannually from seed sown in early April. The seed was sown, not in a drill but in small groups, four seeds to a six-inch square, leaving a foot space between each group. If all four seeds germinated, they would be thinned to one, sometimes two, if both were very strong. This method enabled us to dig up strong crowns to plant in the permanent beds. Before replanting took place the old soil was carted away and replaced by a compost made up of four parts of good turfy loam, one part of leaf mould, one part of well rotted manure, and to each bushel of compost, a six-inch pot of coarse sand and a six-inch pot of medium bonemeal, all thoroughly mixed together. The shoots from the new crowns were not harvested for three years and to ensure that this rule was rigidly enforced the new crowns were distinguished by markers in the form of canes painted white.

We grew three varieties of artichokes, Jerusalem, Chinese and the Globe. Jerusalem artichokes are grown in a similar manner to potatoes, their foliage rapidly reaches a height of eight to ten feet, and provides a useful screen for the protection of other plants.

Chinese artichokes, to give them their correct title, *Stachys tuberifera*, only reach a height of fifteen to eighteen inches. Small tubers are planted four inches deep and one foot apart in rows two feet apart. The plant produces small white odd-shaped tubers which when cooked and served with a butter sauce are considered to be a delicacy.

Globe artichokes are not so widely known, but not only are they a delicious vegetable, they also provide a very decorative plant for the herbaceous border. In view of this it is rather surprising that one rarely sees the plant growing in the average small garden. We grew the plant chiefly for the flower heads which are formed of fleshy scales. When they were fully developed but before the scales opened they were cut with a few inches of stem. In this state they can be kept, remaining fresh for several days before use in the kitchen where they are cooked until the heads are tender and then served with a butter sauce, or alternatively, after boiling, fried in a savoury batter.

The site for the globe artichokes was well manured and prepared during the late autumn and allowed to settle for planting in April. Propagation was effected by obtaining suckers. After dividing a mature plant in early April, a clump of three suckers is planted, each clump thirty inches apart and from four to five feet between rows. The plants do not produce usable heads until the second year.

Once I remember seeing what I thought was a large untidy coarse cabbage growing in the garden, in fact I was rather surprised to see it grown in a cultivated garden, but one day I was sent to gather the large outer leaves from the plant. I learnt that it was the thick leaf stalk that was used in the kitchen, and it was cooked and served in a manner similar to sea-kale. The name given to this vegetable was *Couve Tronchude*, commonly called Portugal cabbage as it was introduced into England from Traxuda in Portugal in 1821. It was one of the old Squire's favourite dishes, and as far as I remember it was never grown again after his death.

Practically everybody with a vegetable garden grows runner beans, but if you want a very early and prolific crop, or intend to grow for exhibition at one of the early shows, extra special cultivation is needed. This requires an effort but I am sure you will find it well worth while. First an open sunny site should be chosen and a trench dug out fifteen inches deep and three feet wide. Heap the excavated soil on either side of the trench, then a length of subsoil, about a yard, is removed from the trench to a further depth of fifteen inches. This excavated subsoil can be wheeled away as it will not be required. The bottom of this small second trench is dressed with a layer of farmyard manure. When this has been done a further length is dug out, and the soil heaped on the manure in the first length. This operation is repeated until the whole length of the trench has been completed. A second layer of manure is then spread along the length of the trench and lightly forked in and trodden down. Yet a third layer of manure, well rotted this time, is added to the original top soil outside the trench. This mixture is then shovelled back into the trench, lightly trodden down and allowed to settle. This preparation can be carried out at any convenient time during the winter months. In bygone days unlimited quantities of manure were readily available, but as far back as 1915 the motor car began to appear and the horse to disappear, therefore substitutes for horse manure were found, such as lawn mowings and garden refuse rotted down on the compost heap with a generous amount of coarse bonemeal.

The beans are initially grown singly in a sixty size pot

during May, in preparation for planting out as soon as the danger of frost is over. Before planting out, stout poles are driven into the soil, twelve inches apart. The plants are spaced out three feet apart and not six to nine inches apart as most seed catalogues recommend. When the plants have reached a height of two feet, the tops are pinched out and this operation is repeated when the plants have reached the height of four feet. An early crop is ensured because air is able to circulate easily between the plants, allowing the setting of the first crop of flowers, which under normal conditions usually fall off. This method of cultivation also means that a mass of roots are not competing for the food in the compost, and accordingly prolific crops result. Also to help the first crop of flowers to set the plants should be syringed twice each day.

I have seen plants with vines as thick as a man's thumb almost ten feet high and covered with beans, so one can imagine that stout supports really are essential.

The plot allocated to peas at Aynhoe was also trenched, and before sowing, the seed was dressed with red lead. The desired quantity was emptied into a flat tray, lightly syringed and then dusted with red lead, the tray being agitated to allow all the seed to be treated. Whilst this precaution prevented mice from eating the actual seed it did not prevent them from eating the young growth when the seed germinated. To combat this menace I used to collect up rose prunings, especially those with plenty of thorns, and cut them into six-inch lengths and place them across the planted rows. As is the general practice wire netting protected the young peas from birds. On reflection many things which we used to do in those days appear to be extravagant to-day, but it must be remembered that labour was plentiful then and it was the final result, not time that mattered.

We grew twenty-four rows of strawberries, each row being over twenty yards long. The first eight rows were runners planted the previous autumn. These would not be allowed to fruit, and in turn would supply runners for the following year. The next eight rows being second year plants provided the large fruit for dessert, whilst the last provided the fruit for preserving, after which they were grubbed up.

The very late broccoli was planted on the plot vacated by the strawberries, and usually an iron bar was needed to make the holes in which to dib the plants. The reason for planting late broccoli on this firm ground was to enable the plants to grow slowly, thus becoming sturdy and able to withstand a hard winter.

A continual supply of rhubarb was required at Aynhoe to supply the demands from the kitchen, and so three separate plots of ground were allocated for its cultivation. The first plot contained one year old crowns, the second two year old crowns, and the third three and four year old crowns. The method adopted was as follows:—after a vacant plot had been trenched and liberally manured, young crowns having several good buds were selected from the outside of four year old crowns. These were planted three feet apart about two inches deep below the ground during the latter part of February. Thereafter it was only necessary to keep the plot clean and remove any flower stalks that formed until the autumn when a top dressing of manure was spread over the plot ensuring that the crown buds remained exposed. The second plot which had been planted the year before was similarly treated. The third plot was equally divided and one half forced, whilst the remainder provided rhubarb for pulling and supplied strong crowns for the next year's plot. When the rhubarb began to decay in the autumn the required crowns were lifted and then left on the ground exposed to early frosts before they were taken in to be forced. The remaining crowns were forced by covering them with large rhubarb pots. These pots resembled bell-glasses in shape and were covered by lids. They were two feet tall and measured sixteen inches in diameter at the base.

Long after these pots had ceased to be used for forcing rhubarb, my nephew who lived in London came to spend a holiday with us. He was five years old, and my son was four months his junior. One day during his stay I heard some loud screaming. I ran to discover the cause of the commotion and I found my son planting his cousin in one of the pots. He had persuaded his cousin to stand in the giant pot and by the time I arrived on the scene, the pot was almost full of soil and John was busily engaged in firming the soil around his cousin with one of my potting sticks. He had of course spent many hours with me in the greenhouses watching me potting plants.

In a small village between Aynhoe and Banbury, growing rhubarb was big business a hundred years ago. Rhubarb roots were dried and sold to herbalists who used them as a cure for many ills, among them dysentery.

In common with most large gardens of that time there was a mushroom house at Aynhoe, heat being provided by hot water pipes. It measured twenty feet long by ten feet wide and was provided with a narrow path running the length of the house. It had a second ceiling constructed of lengths of wood covered with roofing felt, the area between the two ceilings being packed with straw. There were six separate beds in the house, three tiers on either side of the path. Fresh horse droppings with a little short straw added were brought from the stables and heaped in an adjoining shed. The mixture was then carefully turned on alternate days until the rank smell had left the heap, this usually happened after the third or fourth turning. The mushroom beds were then prepared to a depth of one foot. As soon as the temperature had dropped to between 80 and 85 degrees Fahrenheit, spawn was placed eight inches apart over the surface of the beds. The spawn used came in the shape of a brick and resembled hard peat.

The temperature of the beds was checked twice daily and at the least sign of heat vapour, the surface was pierced to allow the steam to escape. As soon as the danger of overheating had passed, usually after about ten days, the beds were covered with one inch of sifted loam. Sometimes I was instructed to damp down the house and all around apart from the actual beds. The foreman attended to this task and he also gathered the mushrooms although I was allowed to carry the basket. He never cut the mushrooms when gathering but picked them with a little twist. On en-quiring the reason for this, he explained that this method ensured that the solid mass at the base of each mushroom was removed, the small hole left being filled with fresh loam. Cutting meant that the severed stems remained often result-ing in mould and fungus appearing and completely destroy-ing all the remaining mushrooms large or small with which it came into contact.

I thought it better not to enquire whether this is what happened to a bed a month or so before, when a crop of young mushrooms which had just begun to be harvested disappeared overnight. I never learnt what went wrong, but recall I had to clean the bed away and wash the surround-ing area with a soapy fungicide. Remembering the look on the foreman's face when I was instructed to clear the bed, I decided it was wiser not to ask questions.

Some gardens were not as fortunate as we were at Aynhoe and had no mushroom house at their disposal, but neverthe-less they grew mushrooms successfully in the open. The method employed was similar to that followed for indoor cultivation, although the formation of the beds was differ-ent. They needed to be four feet wide at the base, narrowing to a width of four inches at the top. Care was necessary to ensure that the bed was not too narrow, otherwise there was insufficient material to provide a lasting heat, which is so necessary to allow the spawn to run quickly through the bed. The outside beds were well trodden down, and finally finished off with the fork. The spawn was laid two inches below the surface and the whole bed was covered with mats or straw and left undisturbed for just over a week. Then this protection was removed and the bed covered with one inch of good garden soil which was beaten down firmly with the back of the spade, and was finally dressed with long strawy manure from which the horse droppings had been shaken out. In about six weeks the mushrooms appeared.

Mushrooms are plentiful in the shops but anyone living near racing or riding stables might like to experiment with mushrooms in their own back garden using this method.

The Park House was provided with a variety of vegetables all the year round, and so peas, dwarf beans, potatoes and cauliflowers were all grown in pots for early use, as also were strawberries. We grew two batches of strawberries, a start being made in July by taking runners from clean vigorous maiden plants. These plants produced large numbers of runners, but only the strongest were selected. Runners both for forcing and planting in the borders were rooted into three-inch pots. Those selected for forcing were transferred into six-inch pots when well rooted, using a compost of three parts good fibrous loam, and one part cow manure partly dried so that it would pass through a half-inch sieve. To each barrow load of this mixture was added a six-inch pot of bonemeal together with some coarse silver-sand to keep it porous. The pots were placed on an ash bed in an open sunny position and were moved occasionally, thus preventing the roots from penetrating into the ashes. During the latter part of November, the pots were plunged into a bed of ashes in a cold frame. When the first batch of plants was removed from the ashes, the outsides of the pots were scrubbed, and the plants then dipped in an insecticide before being given a rich top dressing and taken into a cool house. I often recall during the month of April looking up at the pots on the shelves where the large red succulent fruits were supported by small forked sticks. The variety grown was Royal Sovereign.

Soon after starting work in the greenhouses I was fascinated by some plants growing in ten-inch pots each bearing long oval purple fruit. They were purple aubergines, commonly known as egg plants. The seed was sown in early January in a temperature of 65 to 70 degrees Fahrenheit, two or three seeds to a three-inch pot. When the seedlings reached a height of half an inch, only the strongest were allowed to grow on and they were given a position near the glass. When they had rooted they were transferred to four and a half-inch pots using a compost of two parts finely chopped loam, one part dried cow manure and one part leaf soil with a small amount of coarse bonemeal. Later they were again repotted into ten-inch pots using a similar compost with the addition of a liberal amount of coarse bonemeal. When the plants were six inches high the growing point was pinched out thus allowing two shoots to grow on. These in turn were stopped so as to produce four shoots, each shoot producing one fruit. When the fruit had formed the plants were fed regularly every ten days with liquid manure or Thompson's vine and plant manure. Apart from Clay's fertiliser this was the only artificial manure used at Aynhoe. When the fruits reached the kitchen, they were cut lengthwise, and after the seeds had been removed were served with melted butter. This plant must have the protection of a glass house, and requires warmth. In fact Gerard, writing on aubergines as long ago as 1595, stated that they grew almost everywhere in Eygpt, and brought forth fruit as big as cucumbers, but when they were tried in London gardens they failed due to our climate. Apparently in those days there were no hot houses in which to rear tender plants.

Capsicums were also grown under glass in a similar manner to that of the egg plant. Some of the fruits were used before they turned colour for pickles and sauces, the few that were left to ripen, when gathered, were stored in a dry room until required for flavouring purposes, and making vinegar and cayenne pepper.

Sweet corn, or as it was called in those days Indian corn, was grown in exactly the same way as tomatoes, being raised under glass from seed sown during the first week in April. They were potted in three-inch pots, allowed to harden off, and then planted out on a sheltered sunny border.

In the early days of the first world war there was no mass demand for tomatoes, or indeed for the production of any extra food. This was to come later.

Tomatoes were grown solely to supply the needs of the kitchen. We grew two varieties under glass, namely Best of All and Sunrise. We also grew one variety, Essex Wonder, outside on a sheltered border. Although we used no special-ised treatment in their cultivation we very rarely lost any plants. I think a possible reason for this was that in those days we always incorporated a generous amount of wood ashes and old lime mortar rubble in the compost and right from the seedling stage the plants were watered at ten day intervals with a weak solution of permanganate of potash.

Even if the plants became leggy before planting, something that no good gardener allows to happen to-day, we did not worry, we simply planted them at an angle, or in other words, layered them, after first removing the lower leaves. The stem we planted under the soil, leaving the growing shoot and a few leaves above ground level near the stake to which the plant was eventually tied.

CHAPTER SEVEN

Fruits Out of Doors

A LARGE VARIETY OF FRUIT WAS GROWN IN THE gardens, apples particularly being in abundance. They were grown as standards in the orchard and as bush and cordon trained in the kitchen garden. On the east and west garden walls, which were built of brick and about twelve feet high, plum and pear trees were trained.

Morello cherries occupied the north wall which was also the back wall of the long peach house, whilst the walls facing south used to support a range of fruit houses. On an outside wall facing north and opposite the bothy were trained trees of currants and gooseberries. These naturally ripened late, and thus formed a welcome change as dessert fruit.

In the very early days, before I started work, the dessert fruit which reached the dining room at the Park House was accompanied by small cards naming the various varieties. This apparently was the general procedure among the gentry, and would lead to discussion amongst the guests on the merits of the fruit provided, and comparisons would be made with the fruits grown in their own gardens.

While it was the duty of the gardener in charge of the kitchen garden to deliver the fruit and vegetables to the kitchen, it was my task to take the dessert fruit direct to the butler's pantry. There was an understanding between the butler and Mr. Brown the head gardener that no fruit should be placed on the dinner table a second time. Consequently the fruit left over was the butler's to dispose of as he wished. It was usually distributed to the house-keeper's room, the servants' hall, and of course some of it found its way into his own household.

We grew the same variety of plum on both the east and west side of the garden walls, and were able to provide a fine dish of dessert plums from July to November.

One variety we grew was Kirke's Blue, a very fine dessert plum bearing large fruit with a golden flesh, and of a very rich flavour. Although it was a rather shy bearer, it was too good to omit on that account. For some obscure reason mice were apt to take a particular liking to this plum and we were always obliged to take steps to combat this menace.

A fruit which received special attention at Aynhoe was the pear *Doyenne du Comice* which is generally recognised to be the most delicious of all pears, its flesh being exceptionally sweet and melting. Trees of this variety were planted against both the east and west walls, and also in other sheltered parts of the kitchen garden, where they were grown as bush trees in a pyramid form. Close by, trees of Laxton's Superb and Winter Nelis were planted to act as pollinators. During early spring three inches of top soil was removed from beneath the trees, and replaced by a compost, consisting of equal parts of good fibrous loam and old mushroom manure, plus some crushed mortar rubble. Finally the soil was given a thorough mulching with well rotted cow manure. On warm sunny days when the trees were in bloom they were syringed to assist fertilisation. If necessary the roots were also soaked. During the month of October the fruit was tested. We regularly handled it and applied a short upward movement, when the fruit, if ripe for picking, would separate easily from the joint in the stalk. This operation was repeated daily until all the fruit was gathered.

I recall that I was not allowed to touch the fruit during harvesting, instead I carried fruit boxes lined with protective wadding, into which the fruit was placed before being conveyed to the fruit room, where it was stored on shelves. The fruit on the top shelves ripened first, and on the lower shelves last.

Approximately three weeks after gathering, some of the fruit would be ripe enough for the dinner table. To ensure that it was at its best and suitable for eating, each fruit was carefully held in the palm of the hand, and with the nail of the little finger of the other hand pressed lightly near the nose or blossom end. If the nail penetrated easily, the fruit was ready, if not it would be similarly tested a few days later.

We grew many different varieties of apples both for cooking and dessert purposes. Three varieties I recall which I have not seen in recent years are worthy of note. One dessert apple called William Crump had a very rich flavour and was the result of a cross between Cox's Orange Pippin and Worcester Pearmain. The second called Gascoyne Scarlet was the finest coloured apple I have ever known and was chiefly grown for exhibition. The third of these varieties, also grown mainly for exhibition, was Peasgood's Nonsuch. The fruit was large and the flesh soft and juicy. It was also one of the parents of Rev. W. Wilks, one of the best early cooking apples grown at Aynhoe. Of the other apples grown at Aynhoe one of the most unusual was Adam's Pearmain, a dessert apple which was pear shaped. The skin golden, flecked with red, the flesh crisp with a rich flavour, it was among the oldest varieties grown at Aynhoe, and was known to have been grown there during the mid 1800's. Another was Hanwell Souring, a first class cooking apple and a very late keeper, lasting well into May, by which time it was excellent for dessert purposes. The fruit was medium to large with yellow skin tinted red, and was of local origin, having been raised at Hanwell, a hamlet two miles north of Banbury. An exceptionally tall tree, the origin of which remained a mystery, grew to a height of over thirty feet. It had a slender trunk, the first branches being fifteen feet from the ground level. The golden coloured fruit was very juicy and sweet, and was at its best when eaten immediately after it was harvested. A large fruit net was erected beneath the tree and I was required to visit the tree several times a day armed with a small butterfly net attached to a long pole to collect the fallen fruit. Wasps which were always trouble-some took a particular liking to this tree and frequently devoured whole apples leaving only the outer skin as a kind of shell. Unfortunately this unique tree was uprooted during a gale in 1921.

Surprising although it may seem we were not troubled by pests in those days to the extent that we are to-day. No doubt this was because all fruit trees outside were sprayed during the winter months with a tar oil wash and again during the spring with a copper compound called Mardol, or alternatively with Lime Sulphur. One year however American Blight was very prevalent. The fruit had already formed on the trees. To control this menace I prepared a paraffin emulsion, using 1 pound of soft soap, which I placed in a bucket and covered with paraffin. For the next hour I patiently stirred the mixture with a piece of wood. This is the only safe way to make paraffin emulsion and it is surpris-ing how much paraffin the soap absorbs. Finally the surplus paraffin is poured away and the mixture dissolved in one gallon of water. With this solution I painted the trunk and boughs, taking particular care not to impregnate the young shoots or leaves as the paraffin properties in the liquid would have scorched and eventually killed them. For a good cheap insecticide for general purposes use half a pound of soft soap with as much paraffin as it will absorb and then add three gallons of water. The following year there was only an odd patch or so of blight on the trees and this was treated with methylated spirits.

Looking back to those early years the fight against garden pests and the prevention of diseases by cleanliness seemed to be the key-note, but of course one must remember that labour was plentiful.

During the hot summers wasps were extremely troublesome, especially when the fruit was ripening on the walls. One of my tasks was to partly fill a number of wine bottles with beer sweetened with brown sugar. These receptacles were suspended along the walls and each morning the contents of the bottles were emptied into a bucket through a fine sieve, which trapped the dead insects, allowing the mixture to be used again, occasionally being replenished with some fresh beer. We were also encouraged to locate wasps' nests situated within a mile of the gardens, and we were rewarded with a shilling for each one destroyed. Cyanide was used for this purpose. Once we discovered a nest lying in a mole run by the side of the grass path. In fact we could see the actual comb. Having no cyanide available and being unable to destroy the nest with fire because of its proximity to outbuildings, four gardeners armed with besoms set out early one morning and vigorously attacked the nest, whilst I agitated the centre of the nest with a long cane. This operation continued until all wasps were killed and the remarkable thing was that no one was stung. Finally the comb was dug out and then destroyed with the back of a spade.

One year we had an exceptionally large harvest of apples and by the time we gathered the late apples, the fruit room had already been filled. To overcome this problem I was instructed to examine each apple carefully and select the soundest fruits for storage in clamps in much the same way as potatoes are preserved. A half-inch mesh wire frame was placed between two layers of straw before the clamp was covered with soil. The buried apples kept perfectly until the early varieties were used up and space in the fruit room became available. The first apples taken from the pit were perfect specimen fruits of Blenheim Orange which had been gathered from the topmost branches of established trees about a hundred years old. A fortnight or so before Christmas, Mr. Brown decided to dispatch some Blenheims to Covent Garden Market, the fruit being carefully packed in the same manner as peaches. They were of such fine quality that they realised 6d each which was a remarkable price in those days.

During my history lessons at school we learnt of the Battle of Blenheim, and these events were of special interest to me as Blenheim Palace is situated less than twenty miles from Aynhoe. I have therefore a particular interest in the apple Blenheim Orange and I have discovered some interesting facts about it.

George Kempster, a tailor of Woodstock, first grew the apple. He noticed a small seedling growing near a wall and potted and transplanted it. Years later he picked twenty-four bushels of apples from the same tree, which was still standing in 1826. The apple was introduced to the Palace table by the Palace gardener, Mr. Whitman, in 1811, and the first fruits were sold in Covent Garden Market in 1820. In 1822, a Mr. Farrow of Woodstock exhibited five apples weighing just over five and a half pounds, and was awarded a Banksian Medal.

I understand that a Mr. Keene of Fittleworth, Sussex, has a wax replica of a twenty-four ounce Blenheim Orange apple grown in 1822 by a Mr. Griffin of Deddington, a village three miles west of Aynhoe.

During the latter part of the nineteenth century and right up to the first world war Mr. Brown was allowed the sum of £500 a year to run the gardens. Whenever there was a surplus of garden produce after the requirements at the Park House had been met, he was at liberty to sell this produce thus raising funds which he could use to purchase items to supplement the supplies to the house whenever there was a shortage of a particular commodity in the garden, although usually this problem did not arise as it was the custom of head gardeners to help each other at these times. If for instance a special party was being held at the Park House and Mr. Brown did not have sufficient ripe peaches to meet the requirements, his friends would come to his assistance and vice-versa.

In any event nothing was wasted and any surplus produce was distributed amongst the old people and local hospitals, and baskets filled with apples and pears were dispatched to the village school to be shared among the school children.

Among other fruit bearing trees grown at Aynhoe were the mulberry, medlar, quince and fig. Figs were grown against sheltered walls facing south or west. We grew two varieties. Brown Turkey, the fruit of which was rich and sugary and ripened early, was an abundant bearer, one of the hardiest of the species, and considered to be the best variety for outdoor cultivation. The second variety, equally hardy, was named Brunswick, although it was not quite so richly flavoured as Brown Turkey.

The mulberry was grown not only for its fruit, but also as a decorative tree in the pleasure grounds. The Squire delighted in eating the ripe mulberries as he strolled around the grounds, and also it was a very popular fruit in the kitchen at the House.

The fruit of the medlar is unsuitable for dessert purposes until it begins to decay, and indeed after the death of the old Squire I cannot recall any occasion when the fruit was even gathered.

The quince, which is pear shaped, is generally used for flavouring and making a rather exquisite jelly with a distinct flavour of its own.

Of course there was also the apricot, a fruit with which I have been associated throughout my gardening career, and a fruit which has a special association with Aynhoe, for Aynhoe is widely referred to as the *Apricot Village*.

This title came about because the majority of the houses in the village, with walls facing south or west, have apricot trees trained along them. Apricots have always flourished in the village because the natural soil is a stony, sandy marl with a plentiful supply of lime. Lime is of course most essential in the cultivation of all stone fruit, as indeed is an abundant supply of water at the root, and this was provided both from the many natural springs in the village, and from the rain water running from the roofs of the cottages, the surplus water draining away down the hill into the valley below.

The fact that the village was located on a hillside sloping to the south and west meant that the air was drier there, and therefore when the trees were in bloom they escaped many of the late frosts, and whenever any of the blooms were affected by the frost, their position on either a south or west wall ensured that they had time to thaw out before being exposed to early sunlight.

We discovered that apricots did not fare so well in the cultivated kitchen gardens at the Park House. This was because the soil was too rich, and in addition, the flat terrain of these gardens denied the trees sufficient water. We found that the trees would grow vigorously for a few years, but then the branches would begin to die back, and the fruit yield became very poor.

I recall that during my early days in the gardens, to encourage the continuity of the legend of the apricot village, trees specially trained on a six foot leg were supplied by Messrs. Dickson of Chester. These trees were planted along a wall in the gardens, and whenever one of the trees in the village showed signs of dying, it was replaced from this new stock, the variety being Moorpark, which was probably also the variety of the old trees, although some say they were from a strain known as Breda.

Upon my appointment as head gardener, the trees became my responsibility. Life in the village was rapidly changing, and it was no longer the practice to send the fruit from the trees to the Park House, and so when a tree needed replacing, it would be effected on the understanding that the occupier of the cottage concerned undertook to care for and train the tree properly in exchange for which he was entitled to the fruit. In the few instances where the trees did become neglected, we would take over the care of the tree, and accordingly when the time came we would claim the fruit. In those days it was possible to enforce

such a system as the whole village belonged to the Cartwright family. Subsequently, however, with the ever increasing traffic passing through the village, car owners
began stealing the fruit at night, some going to the trouble
of standing on the roofs of their vehicles in order to reach
the topmost fruit. As a result the cottagers began to lose
interest, and we were no longer in a position to be able to
impose conditions, being only too pleased to be able to
plant a tree when necessary, in the hope that a good crop of
fruit would encourage the occupier to help look after the
tree.

There was further cause for concern when, during the
pre-war years, guttering was erected beneath the roofs of
the houses to enable the rainwater to be directed into the
several drains. Furthermore, the paths which had been
hitherto cobbled were replaced with concrete. These changes
meant that there was a lack of surface water to feed the
trees, and subsequently blank spaces began to appear on
the walls of the cottages.

However, many of the parishioners did persevere, and
gave the extra attention necessary to their trees, and at the
time of writing I am pleased to be able to record that the
blank spaces are being filled by trees supplied by Mr. H. J.
Phillips of the Northamptonshire Institute of Agriculture.
With the addition of these new trees, I have no doubt that
Aynhoe will soon regain its fame as the *Apricot Village*.

So much for the apricot's connection with Aynhoe, and
now a little about its history and cultivation. The apricot is a
native of Manchuria and Northern China, in which countries
it is supposed to have been cultivated many hundreds of
years before Christ. It is generally believed that this fruit
was first introduced into this country from Italy in 1524 by
the gardener to King Henry VIII, a certain Mr. Wolff.

Of the two varieties grown at Aynhoe, Breda was a hardy,
good cropping variety. Its medium-sized fruit is both
tender and sweet. It has been known in this country for
several centuries, and could well be the variety introduced
to England by Mr. Wolff.

Moorpark is a hardy and vigorous variety. Its fruit is very juicy and exceptionally large, particularly when the young fruit has been properly thinned. From reading up some of the old fruit catalogues it would appear that the present day apricot Moorpark is derived from the variety either raised or introduced by Lord Anson in 1760 at Moor Park, Hertfordshire. This however was not the first time it is said to have been introduced into this country.

Sir William Temple, who was born in 1628, introduced Moorpark from Brussels where he lived in 1652, but no one is quite certain whether he named it after his own garden Moor Park, then spelt More Park, at Farnham in Surrey, or another that he admired and wrote about enthusiastically, Moor Park in Hertfordshire. Although these two reports were separated by more than 100 years, I feel there must be some connection.

The R.H.S. have been most helpful in sending me the following extract from Robert Hoggs' *Fruit Manual* 5th Ed: 1884.

The Moor Park Apricot is said by some to have been introduced by Lord Anson from the Continent and planted at Moorpark, near Watford in Hertfordshire. By others, its introduction is ascribed to Sir Thomas More, who in the beginning of the last century is also said to have planted it at Moorpark; and a third account is that Sir William Temple introduced it. But by whomsoever it was raised or introduced, or at what period, it is quite certain it was very little known till late in the century. Neither Hitt nor Miller notices it in any edition of their works. I do not find it mentioned in any of the Brompton Park catalogues before 1784 when it is called Temple Apricot. In 1788 it is first called Moorpark. In 1784 it was cultivated to the extent of three rows, or 300 plants, but in 1797 that quantity was increased to thirty-five rows or 3,500 plants.

These facts are of immense interest to me, partly because I have a Silver Hogg Medal in my possession.

Fan training is the best method of growing apricots, mainly because this obviates the risk of branches dying back. Also, it is advisable to allow young growth to remain at the base of the main branches, as this allows any vacancies to be filled. However, it must be borne in mind that it is equally wrong to crowd the tree, and careful pruning and disbudding are essential. These operations are exactly the same as the methods used in the cultivation of the peach, the only difference being that the apricot forms fruit spurs on the older wood, whereas the peach does not. The finest of all is produced on a one year old shoot.

As I have already mentioned, apricots require plenty of water at the roots and so, to ensure that they receive a sufficient quantity, a method which I have adopted is worthy of note: Normally when a can of water is emptied at the base of a tree trained against a wall, the majority runs away and is wasted. This can be remedied by partly sinking a six-inch drain pipe either side of the tree, (see page 66). It is a simple matter to empty a can of water into these receptacles, thus ensuring that sufficient water reaches the roots. The same method can be utilised when the trees require a little extra food in liquid form. This method of watering can also apply to roses and other shrubs.

I have included below some recipes for apricots which may be of use if you are lucky enough to have apricots available.

APRICOT CREAM

12 ripe apricots
½ lb. sugar
1½ pints milk
the yolks of 5 eggs
1 oz. of gelatine

Divide the fruit and take out the stones. Boil them in a syrup made from ¼ lb. sugar and ¼ pint of water until they form a thin marmalade. Rub through a sieve and set aside. Boil the milk with the other ¼ lb. of sugar—let it cool a little then mix it well with the yolks of eggs which have been previously well beaten. Put this mixture into a jug. Place the jug in hot water and stir it all one way over the heat until it thickens—on no account let it boil. Strain through a sieve and add 1 oz. gelatine previously melted with a small quantity of water. Keep stirring till nearly cold. Mix the cream with the apricots. Stir well and put it into an oiled mould. Let the mixture set in the refrigerator before turning out.

APRICOT BOUCHÉES

6 fresh apricots
some puff pastry
loaf sugar
¼ pint of cream

Stamp out small rounds of pastry and make a smaller indentation with a round cutter about the size of the fruit. Sift over powdered sugar and bake a nice brown in a quick oven.

Cut each fresh fruit in half—remove stones and boil fruit in syrup made from loaf sugar and a little water till tender.

When the pastry comes out from the oven, depress lightly in the centre of each piece to make room for the fruit.

When both pastry and fruit are cold, lay half an apricot hollow upwards and fill with whipped cream.

APRICOT CONSERVE

To 4 lb. of fresh fruit allow 3 lb. sugar. Choose good sound fruit slightly under-ripe. Wipe them—cut in halves with a silver knife—remove the stones.

Spread them in layers with the sugar and allow to stand all night.

Break some of the stones—remove the kernel—blanch them and sprinkle over the fruit.

Next day place into the preserving pan and bring slowly to the boil stirring all the time. Simmer until the fruit turns clear and this easy recipe will provide a delicious jam of extraordinary flavour which can be used for special occasions.

COMPOTE OF APRICOTS

½ pint syrup
12 green apricots

Make the syrup as previously described—whilst still boiling put in the apricots and simmer gently for 15-20 mins. taking care not to let them break. Arrange them in a glass dish and when cool pour over the syrup and serve cold. For 4-5 people. Very good.

APRICOTS À L'AMBASSADRICE

6-8 large ripe but firm apricots
1 piece vanilla pod—¾ oz. gelatine
2 eggs—1 tablespoon Maraschino
½ pint syrup—½ pint cream—1 gill milk
½ oz. castor sugar—1 slice pineapple—a few ripe cherries

Cut the apricots in halves and remove the stones. Cook very carefully in the syrup with the vanilla pod. When done place through a sieve and drain—skins can be removed. Boil up the milk and whisk in 2 well beaten yolks of eggs. Add the gelatine—previously melted—and the sugar, then strain into a basin.

Whip the cream and add about half to the custard when cool enough.

Cut the pineapple into small dice. Stone the cherries and slice them. Sprinkle over the Maraschino.

Mix these within the prepared cream and pour into a flat, fluted, round sandwich mould, then place on ice to set. When set, unmould onto a decorative dish and arrange the apricots neatly on top of the shape. Fill the centre with whipped cream. Glaze the apricots and finally decorate with glacé cherries and angelica. A very good dessert.

CHAPTER EIGHT

Fruits Under Glass

FIFTY YEARS AGO THERE WERE SIX HOUSES OF vines grown at Aynhoe. I was fortunate to have the benefit of working under an expert on all forms of fruit, and later during my visits to Woburn Abbey Gardens I had the advantage of watching some of the finest grapes I have ever seen being grown.

The varieties we grew at Aynhoe were Alicante, Foster's Seedling, Gros Colman, Madresfield Court and Muscat of Alexandria.

The easiest grape to grow especially in a cold greenhouse is Black Hamburgh. It is a free flowering vigorous variety, and will even succeed in the open air in sheltered warm situations, and it is especially valuable for furnishing a verandah facing south or west.

Although it was not grown at Aynhoe when I began work there, it had at one time, prior to my arrival, been one of their best early forcing varieties in the heated greenhouses.

Another variety suitable for a slightly heated greenhouse is Madresfield Court, an early grape of great merit. The bunches are large, long and tapering, the berries black, covered with the most beautiful bloom when ripe. Considerable skill is required when handling this grape in preparation for the dinner table or for the exhibition bench if the bloom is to be left intact. The slightest mark on the bloom of any of the fruit can easily cost an exhibitor the first prize. In certain seasons and under certain conditions the berries are inclined to crack during the ripening process, and to help obviate this a current of warm air should be kept circulating through the house. To do this the hot water pipes must always be kept warm, and air admitted through the top and bottom ventilators both day and night. We also covered the inside borders with a layer of straw to prevent any moisture rising and the outside borders were covered in case of a heavy downpour.

In my opinion the finest and best flavoured of all grapes is Muscat of Alexandria. It is however more difficult to grow than most varieties, and requires special attention to bring it to perfection. It is an old variety and as its name would imply is of North African origin, where it was known as Zibibbu. It is a large grape and vigorous in growth. The bunches are large and tapering and the skin of the berries is rather thick and a pale shade with a somewhat thin bloom. The flesh is exceedingly rich and has a very pronounced and delicious musk flavour. This variety will only succeed in a heated greenhouse, and is a notoriously shy setter requiring special care at that time. The gentle tapping of the rods is sufficient to cause free dispersion of the pollen on all free setting varieties, but in the case of shy setters such as Muscat of Alexandria, artificial means are necessary. For this purpose a rabbit's tail tied to a cane or a fine camel hair brush can be utilised, and to make the operation more successful, pollen from a free setting variety like the Black Hamburgh can beneficially be used. Should the latter flower earlier than the muscat, its pollen may be shaken or brushed off into a cardboard box and kept dry ready for use at the required time. It will retain its potency for several weeks. One of the causes of sterility in grapes is the presence of a gummy substance on the top of the stigma. To remove this, the bunches of fruit must be syringed early in the morning with tepid rain water and then allowed to dry before the flowers are fertilised.

Anyone interested in cultivating a vine can purchase a young dormant rod from a reliable firm. After planting, it requires to be cut to a height of about five feet. During the second year the strongest leading shoot must be trained for further development of the vine. The side shoots are then tied in horizontally and interspersed alternately on each side of the main rod about nine to twelve inches apart. In autumn the side shoots are shortened to two buds, and these become the formation of the spurs. The leading growth is also stopped at a length of five feet, thus leaving a vine of about ten feet overall length. The following year the vine is similarly treated and if it is growing vigorously a couple of bunches of fruit may be allowed to remain and ripen. Thereafter as soon as the leaves fall pruning must take place, again ensuring that all young growths from the spurs are cut back to two buds.

Many people are perplexed by the problem of how to thin the bunches when the berries have begun to swell. The number of bunches allowed to flower and set is too often in excess of the quantity required to form a crop. Of course the number of bunches finally allowed to remain depends largely upon the health and constitution of the vine. I suggest that one bunch to each foot of rod is ideal. The thinning of the free setting varieties can take place as soon as they are set, but in the case of muscats, it is advisable to allow the berries to swell a little before they are thinned as by that time the more promising berries can be more easily perceived.

The general form of the bunch is a main stalk at the base of which the individual berries spring direct. Above this point small stems branch out, each stem bearing three berries, a terminal berry and one either side. A little higher up the stalk the stems become larger and towards the top of the bunch they in turn throw out little stems forming shoulders.

Thinning in its initial stages consists of cutting out the innermost berries nearest the main stalk. This allows the outer berries extra space in which to grow, whereas if they were removed and the berries nearest the stem allowed to remain, the bunch would still be crowded. The next stage entails removing the two side berries on each branch, thus leaving the terminal berries only. When the berries begin to increase in size the bunches can be regulated by a further thinning and when the fruit has eventually reached the stoning stage and is almost fully developed, the bunches must be carefully examined to ensure that none of the berries have become wedged together, bearing in mind that the ultimate aim is a well shaped bunch without being over-crowded. During the final growing period the shoulder part of the bunch can be lifted up with a wide piece of raffia tied to a support above the bunch. This method is also a great help when thinning the shoulders.

A useful hint for someone who is new to growing grapes is to experiment with the discarded bunches when learning the thinning out process. Specially designed vine scissors must be used to avoid touching the sensitive berries with the hands.

The vine is susceptible to various diseases, the chief of which are mildew, shanking, scalding and rust; among the insect enemies are mealy bug, scale, thrips, red spider and wasps. These I will deal with in a later chapter.

Anyone who is able to grow tomatoes, and the usual run of greenhouse plants, will not find it difficult to grow grapes, although he may not find it quite as profitable. To-day the market for tomatoes has been virtually captured by the market gardener and foreign growers, who are able to flood the market at most times of the year. They do not have the same flavour as those grown in our own green-houses, but the same can be said of the grape, and therefore in my opinion, grapes are a better proposition than tomatoes, not merely for the fruit, but from a decorative point of view. There is nothing particularly attractive about tomatoes, especially when grown in a verandah or conservatory, but the same cannot be said of the grape. Enormous satisfaction and pleasure can be derived from the attractively shaped soft green leaves, the scent of the flowers, the changing colour of the berries, and the autumn colouring of the leaves, to say nothing of the shade afforded by the vine when relaxing in the verandah.

You will have gathered by now that the vine requires a considerable amount of attention and care. I will endeavour briefly to sum up and to outline the methods of cultivation which we employed at Aynhoe, commencing from the period which immediately follows the gathering of the berries.

After the bunches have been cut, the strong growths should be shortened to half their original length. This helps to 'plump up' the buds, only the weaker growths being tipped and left until the fall of the leaf.

When the leaves have fallen, prune back to two buds, and then thoroughly cleanse the rods, making certain to remove all loose bark. Having done this, wash carefully with an insecticide.

Before growth appears on the vines, the borders should be examined and if necessary given a thorough soaking. The rods should then be freed from their supports and tied down in a half circle; this operation has the effect of checking the flow of sap, thus allowing the buds to break evenly. As soon as the buds have burst and started into growth, the rods should be tied back to their supports, whereupon attention should be concentrated on disbudding, stopping and tying.

The vines should be disbudded gradually, in order that the most promising shoot should remain on each spur. Where the spurs are found to be very far apart, both shoots may remain, and should be stopped at the second leaf beyond the bunch, all superfluous bunches being removed.

The tying down of the growths must be done gradually, otherwise the whole shoots will break off at the spur. All sub-lateral growths appearing below the bunch should be rubbed out, and those beyond the bunch should be stopped at the first joint until there is an even spread of leaves covering the trellis supports.

The treatment of the borders, composition of the soil, and the cleansing of the vineries, are all matters with which I shall deal in the chapter on peaches, the methods being identical.

Before leaving the story of the grape, I must relate one of my early experiences in the vineries, which illustrates my description of the distinct flavour of the muscat. On this particular occasion we had been required to keep the grapes back for as long as possible after they were ripe. After a while some of the berries began to shrivel and turn brown so that they resembled raisins. One late December morning I was engaged in cutting out these raisins before they began to decay. The morning was a sunny one, and this, together with the warmth from the hot water pipes, made the atmosphere rather close. As I cut away the shrivelled berries, I began tasting them and I found them quite pleasant, in fact similar to a sip of wine. I continued to enjoy this new form of refreshment whilst cutting away the berries, until suddenly I began to feel dizzy. Putting this down to the warm atmosphere, I walked outside into the fresh air, whereupon my legs buckled beneath me, and I realised that I had become drunk for the first time in my life.

Pineapples were grown at Aynhoe during the last century in a special house known as the Pine Stove. This lean-to house, just over forty feet long, faced south and was situated at the north end of the frame yard. It was sheltered from the north winds by a large peach house. It vaguely resembled a deep frame sunk into the ground. Heat which was essential was supplied by hot beds and by a nine-inch flue built into the brick walls which supported the pineapple beds. The heat and gas fumes escaped through a tall chimney. To help retain the warmth during cold spells, mats were placed over the roof. A waterproof sheet was then spread over the mats and tied down, thus preventing them from blowing away, and at the same time keeping them dry. This Pine Stove was converted into a span-roofed house during the latter part of the nineteenth century.

As a young boy I thought pineapples grew on trees, a popular misconception amongst young people. On learning of my mistake I became very interested about their cultivation and I gleaned some useful information about them from the old gardeners. The compost in which they were grown consisted of two parts fibrous loam, one part leaf soil and one part deer droppings, with a liberal sprinkling of crushed bones and old mortar rubble. They were propagated by means of suckers from old fruiting plants taken after the fruit had been cut. This was the usual method, although sometimes the crown of the fruit was taken and rooted in early spring in a temperature of 80 degrees Fahrenheit. The pineapple likes plenty of liquid manure, such as stable drainings, cow, sheep, deer or poultry droppings and occasionally soot water. Top dressing, which is necessary as the feeding action of the roots, evaporation and frequent watering all tend to exhaust the food in the original compost, was carried out periodically.

Although I have never actually grown pineapples, I have grown melons, and during the first few years of my gardening career, they were considered to be equal in importance to grapes and peaches, and so care was taken to grow them to perfection. They were in fact grown in the old Pine House which by then had been converted into a span-roofed house which was referred to as the Little Stove.

Melons can be grown to a fair size in a warm house without sun-heat, but the fruits will not ripen properly without the influence of the sun. No amount of artificial heat will effect the conversion of the crude juices of the fruit into saccharine matter and give it the delicious flavour of a melon ripened by the sun and cut fresh from the vine. For this reason we grew our melons on the sunny south side of the house. They will survive without bottom heat, but will do much better with it, and this heat can be supplied either by a hot bed or water pipes.

During the conversion of the old Pine House a boiler

and hot water system was installed, the chimney stack still being utilised. A flow pipe from the boiler situated just beneath the eaves on the north side returned to the boiler via the water tank. On the south side there was a flow and return pipe beneath the melon bed and another resting on the old flue wall. Consequently it was comparatively easy to maintain a temperature of around 80 degrees Fahrenheit. Valves were placed adjacent to the partition between the two sections of the house in order that one section might be maintained at a slightly lower temperature than the other, thus ensuring a succession of ripe fruit over a longer period.

The bed in which the melons grew was supported by a platform about twelve inches above the hot water pipes. Spaces were left between the boards forming the platform to allow the warmth from the pipes to penetrate into the bed.

Anyone who has sampled only the imported melons purchased from his local greengrocer would be very pleasantly surprised by the different flavour of those grown properly in a greenhouse, and because I feel that some of my readers might like to grow melons for themselves, I will write describing the method used not only at Aynhoe, but at Woburn Abbey Gardens nearly fifty years ago.

A heated greenhouse is of course essential, and it is a simple task to partition a small section off with polythene sheets which can be fixed with drawing pins.

Good rich turfy loam is needed, to which must be added a liberal amount of old lime mortar rubble, in fact any soil that generates canker should have lime added to it. Melons are subject to canker and should it appear, it should be lightly scraped out and the cut surface covered with lime.

In by-gone days pigeon dung was added to the loam, this being the mixture used in Eastern Countries for many centuries, and of course very few large establishments were without a pigeon or dovecote in those days.

I can still recall the first time I saw melons growing, and will always remember the rich perfume of the ripe melons which greeted me as I entered the greenhouse.

To ensure that the melons are ripe by the beginning of July, the seed is sown singly in small pots during early February. The pots are then sunk into a hot bed or propagating case with a bottom heat of 70 to 75 degrees Fahrenheit. As soon as the seedlings appear they are removed from the propagating case and allowed to harden off for one or two days before they are placed as near the glass as possible. A night temperature of 70 degrees Fahrenheit must be maintained. The plants must be staked out as early as possible, and watered with care. The prepared soil in which the plants are grown consists of a layer of turves grass side down on the platform surface and also a further two layers of turves around the perimeter of the bed only. This leaves a cavity fifteen to eighteen inches wide along the centre of the bed. This space is filled with a prepared compost consisting of broken up fibrous loam, a small amount of old mortar rubble and wood ashes or small charcoal, and a six-inch pot full of coarse bonemeal to each barrow-load, the whole being thoroughly mixed and allowed to stand for a few days to become completely warmed through.

A trellis is required on which to train the plants. Before planting, canes are pushed into the soil and fixed to the bottom wire of the trellis, fifteen inches apart. The plants having been well rooted in forty-eight size pots are then transplanted, one to each cane, sufficient compost being used to cover the ball and be mounded up around each plant. The plants require no water for a day or so, but should be lightly syringed twice daily to combat the red spider menace. Melons will not tolerate cold draughts and therefore special care must be excercised with ventilation. When the plants have progressed, all lateral growths should be removed as far as the lowest trellis wire. From then on all laterals should be stopped one leaf beyond the fruit to prevent overcrowding the foliages. These operations must not be left until a knife needs to be used, and should be carried out at a stage when a nip with the thumb and finger will suffice, because otherwise there is a tendency for the melons to die back and the laterals to canker. Setting the flowers should be carried out around midday, and as melons bear both male and female flowers on the same plant, the former are essential for the fertilisation of the latter and sufficient flowers must be maintained for that purpose. Pollination is carried out by removing a mature male flower, taking off the petals, and transferring the pollen to the stigma of the female flower. The atmosphere must remain fairly dry until the process of setting is over.

The melon foliage is rather tender and should be lightly shaded during the hottest part of the day to prevent scorching, although when the plant becomes mature, it will readily stand the sun, unless very hot sunshine follows a long dull spell. When the fruit is set, two or three should be left to each plant, and it is important that they are set at the same time, because if one is set before the other it will swell so rapidly that the remaining fruits will be inferior or drop off altogether.

When the fruit reaches a considerable size it becomes necessary to support it, because the weight would cause the tender vine to break, and also when the ripening stage is reached the fruit would drop from the stem. In the old days small square containers were suspended from the trellis wires.

However, as far as I can recall, nets were always used at Aynhoe for this purpose, an advantage over the wooden containers which were apt to accumulate moisture where the fruit came in contact with the wood. The cotton nets cost about 3/6 per dozen, and if properly looked after they would remain serviceable for many years.

The fruit should not be allowed to remain until it parts from the stem, but should be cut as soon as cracks appear around the stem and it begins to exude that agreeable perfume so much prized by those who are fond of the fruit. The flavour of most varieties is greatly improved when the fruit is placed on a shelf in an airy room for a week before using.

The variety grown at Aynhoe, Hero of Lockinge, was considered to be the best for small gardens. It was a white fleshed variety which ripened early and kept well. At Woburn Abbey my colleague grew white, scarlet and green fleshed varieties.

One word of warning should any of my readers decide to grow their own melons. Although they require plenty of water while the fruit is swelling, they must not be watered near the collar of the plant, otherwise canker will develop. The mound of soil around the plant is intended to help drain the water away from the stem.

Bananas, oranges and lemons were cultivated at Aynhoe at that time for their ornamental value and I made a start to grow lemons again in 1961 when I was sent a rooted plant of *Citrus ponderosa* which had originated in Florida U.S.A. After three years in a twelve-inch pot it grew to a height of ten feet and bore six lemons, each weighing over twenty ounces, the largest measuring fourteen and a half inches in circumference and weighing twenty-eight ounces. In 1967, I picked one fruit weighing just under two and a quarter pounds.

It may be of help to some of my readers if I briefly explained the meaning of some of the gardening terms in this chapter.

Pollination. Pollination is the act of transferring pollen from the stamens to the pistil. The stamens are the male organs of the flower, the anthers being that part of the stamen producing pollen. The end of the pistil, called the stigma, is the female organ of the flower.

Cross pollination is the act of transferring pollen from one flower to another. This is often done by bees, flies and other insects. Pollen may be transferred in several ways, such as dusting the blooms lightly with a camel hair brush, or a rabbit tail tied to a cane; by hand, using a pair of small tweezers; by jarring or shaking the plant while the pollen on the blooms is dry; by lightly syringing the plant with water.

Fertilisation. The production of seed which will germinate and grow is dependent upon its being fertilised with pollen. When a pollen grain alights upon a stigma in a receptive condition, it grows and sends down a minute tube into the ovary where it makes contact with an embryo seed, and fertilisation takes place.

Stopping. This is the removal of the growing tip of a plant with the object of making it produce side growths, or simply when a growth has reached a desired length. Pinching is removing the growth by hand while the growth is soft and tender.

Disbudding. This is a term applied to the thinning out of unwnated growths. In the case of flowering plants it means removing a number of buds to produce fewer and finer blooms.

Dividing. This means one plant being parted into two or more pieces.

Top Dressing. This is a term used to describe the application of substances into the top surface of the soil, such as prepared compost and artificial fertilisers, lime, etc. Top dressing may consist of bulky substances like farmyard manure, lawn mowings, etc. These however are usually referred to as mulching.

CHAPTER NINE

The First Post War Changes

DURING THE LATTER PART OF 1917 THE EFFECTS of the Great War were being felt. Only one man over military age remained to look after the pleasure grounds, and one other tended the kitchen garden. I was approaching my sixteenth birthday and the greenhouses became my responsibility, sometimes shared by Mr. Brown when he was able to spare the time. One night whilst making my last round I found one of the large plant houses filled with steam, and on investigating I located the cause of the trouble. A leak had developed in one of the top pipes. Not wishing to trouble the head gardener I decided to open the ventilators to release the steam, and then using some clay I partly sealed the leaking pipe, and although this did not altogether stop the water from running out, it did prevent steam from escaping. I then ensured that the feeder for the pipes was filled with water and maintained the boilerfire.

The following morning as it was not possible to obtain the services of a hot water engineer at such short notice we called in the village blacksmith. Finding that part of the pipe was rusted through he made a thin iron patch and after covering the worn part with a mixture of putty and red lead he bolted on the patch with three iron bands. This was merely a temporary measure until such times as a new length of pipe could be obtained. However the replacement never arrived and today, fifty years later, the patch is still intact and has never leaked, which speaks volumes for the skill of the village craftsmen in those days.

In a previous chapter I emphasised the important part that cleanliness plays in keeping down pests and preventing plant diseases. I could also have mentioned care and attention both of which were taken for granted at the turn of the century. But it was a different story during the latter part of the war. Time was the all important factor and consequently the plants did not receive the same care and attention as they had hitherto, and often a pest or disease would be overlooked until the resulting damage was plainly visible.

The most common pest, aphis, was controlled either by spraying with Abol Insecticide or by using a vapouring fumigator. This apparatus, constructed of galvanised steel, had a number of small holes around the sides, and resting on top of a stand fitted over the fumigator was a copper saucer large enough to hold $\frac{1}{8}$ pint of XL All Fumigating Compound, a sufficient amount to fumigate an area of 5,000 cubic feet. To-day the majority of gardeners overcome the pest problem by the use of smoke bombs designed specially for use in the greenhouse. I find however that whilst they kill the majority of pests, a few survive and soon start to breed again, and the species becomes immune. There are of course plants on which certain insecticides must not be used. I have talked this matter over with a gardening colleague of the old school and he and I have both returned to the old remedies. Smoking with Auto Shreds however is an old efficient method of pest control and is still to be recommended.

Thrips, of which there are many species, are most destructive under glass where they will breed at all seasons, particularly if the atmosphere is dry, and arid conditions prevail for any length of time. By good culture and the timely use of the syringe their ravages may be prevented, but so often during those difficult war years this was just what I did not have time to do. Nevertheless I managed to keep the trouble within bounds either by fumigating, and sponging the leaves with Gishurst Compound, or by spraying with a nicotine insecticide.

Mealy bug and scale often became troublesome, especially in one of the vineries where mealy bug really gained a hold, and when this occurred drastic measures had to be employed. Firstly as much foliage as was practicable was cut out and burnt and so also were the bunches of grapes. The border was covered with large sheets of brown paper to prevent the infected foliage coming into contact with the borders. The entire infected matter was then collected and burnt. Later on when the vines became dormant they were pruned back to two buds and the rods scraped to remove all loose bark under which mealy bug was lurking. The house was then made as airtight as possible and fumigated with 2 lbs of sulphur. This operation was carried out by throwing the sulphur onto red hot coke taken from the boiler, and needless to say I vacated the greenhouse rather swiftly. This drastic treatment not only destroyed the mealy bug, but it also blackened the paint work, so that after a thorough wash down the house had to be re-painted. During the following spring and summer a close watch was kept for bugs that had managed to survive; there were a few, and these were easily destroyed by merely touching them with a brush dipped in methylated spirit.

Scale was destroyed by brushing with Gishurst Compound and by fumigating with nicotine. Red spider, despite its name, is not a spider, nor even an insect, it is in fact one of the spinning mites. Dry conditions are most favourable for its multiplication so that water becomes its greatest enemy. If syringing and damping down is done properly this pest is kept under control. If and when red spider attacked the vines, it was the common practice to paint the hot water pipes when the water was fairly hot with a mixture of sulphur and water. On no account was this solution applied to the flues because this would have harmed the vines, having the same effect as burning sulphur on a fire.

Bleeding of vines is usually caused by pruning too late in the season. The sap exudes from the wounds thus caused. Whenever this occurs the wound should be dressed with a styptic, and in any case this can be applied as a precaution. I have also stopped the bleeding with repeated applications of painter's knotting. Once I had great difficulty in stopping the bleeding of a muscat vine. This trouble occurred after the rods had been tied down, when a spur becoming caught in one of the support wires snapped off. I trimmed the break smoothly and covered the wound with styptic. The flow of sap however was too great to allow the styptic to dry and so I heated a flat piece of iron and placed it on the wound, immediately applying the styptic. After a short while the vine began to bleed again and so I repeated the burning treatment, this time using two irons. This appeared to have remedied the trouble, but no, the following morning the wound was still bleeding. This time I decided to use a very old remedy, boiling pitch. I repeated the treatment of the previous day and applied the red hot bars to the wound and then I painted it several times with boiling pitch. Once again a time honoured remedy triumphed over all other methods and the wound was finally sealed.

Mildew, a fungous disease, caused a great deal of worry. I remember I was only sixteen and responsibility was being piled upon me, but I welcomed the challenge, and being of an independant nature I did not continually seek advice from Mr. Brown, but decided to find some of the answers for myself. I discovered the main causes of mildew under glass arose from weak constitution of the plants, poor circulation of air, overcrowding, excessive moisture, and absence of sufficient potash in the soil. Lime is a valuable asset in the soil. I also learnt that when chrysanthemums or roses were allowed to become dry at the root, mildew inevitably resulted. I think that when one has found the source of the trouble a remedy will be found; remedies such as spraying with 1 oz liver of sulphur to 3 gallons of water, or with permanganate of potash diluted to the colour of weak port wine. Another very effective remedy both against mildew and red spider is dusting the plants with flowers of sulphur. This can be done by hand, but is best done by a sulphur vapouriser. The method is quite simple, consisting substantially of heating the sulphur in a vessel having a funnel outlet. The stem is closed with a hollow glass ball, which by rising and falling according to the pressures of hot vapours acts as a safety valve, thereby allowing the escape of sulphur vapour into the air and at the same time preventing the entrance of hot air into the cylinder where it could set fire to the boiling sulphur.

I remember the first time I used a sulphur vapouriser becoming really alarmed when the sulphur began to boil and the vapour rushed out. I felt sure that the whole lot was going to explode as the sulphur was heated by a container burning methylated spirit. When it was only necessary to dust a few plants, a blower known as the Cyclone was used. It was cheap, costing only 2/6d, but effective, and it was very simple to operate requiring the use of one hand only, thus leaving the other free to turn over the plant foliage. Another similar piece of apparatus a little more elaborate than the Cyclone was the Malbex Blower. The original advertisement published in an old catalogue more than sixty years ago, spoke of its process thus:—*The Malbex Blower 10/6d each. A farmer keeps his gun handy to kill his enemies the moment they appear: the Malbex Blower is even more useful and valuable, and should always be kept charged with Sulphur, and at the first sign of mildew, or fungi, or rust, it should be sprinkled and killed just as if it were a lion in the garden. In our opinion this is the most valuable instrument ever invented to make the garden a success. Spray the powder hardly sufficient to be seen, 99 out of 100 persons will use five times more than it needs.*

By using the Malbex Blower you will save crops, otherwise detestable disease will beset the eye when walking round the garden.

Beneath this weighty proclamation appeared a sketch of this deadly weapon, which was in fact a small set of bellows, similar to the bellows which could be found in practically every cottage, except that it was much smaller, and the end of the nozzle pointed upwards. There was a small canister attached to the side to hold the sulphur.

As I have already mentioned, during the early part of 1918 Mr. Brown was able to secure the services of a gardener invalided out of the army. Naturally I welcomed his arrival because by that time all departments of the garden were beginning to show signs of deterioration due to lack of care and attention, unavoidable because of labour shortage, and also due to some extent to lack of experience on my part. Furthermore I soon realised how fortunate I was to be working alongside an expert plantsman and to this day I am reaping the benefit of his advice, for it was he who taught me the value of the various potting composts and how to mix them. He suffered from ear trouble and was inclined to be a little irritable especially if he had to repeat his instructions, and therefore once he had explained to me the ingredients and compositions for a certain compost, he expected me to remember them. From then on and so as to avoid incurring his displeasure I always carried with me a note book in which I faithfully recorded his instructions, making notes of his valuable information. In addition, at the end of each working day I wrote down particulars of all the work carried out during the day and noted anything interesting Mr. Brown might have done. This habit proved invaluable to me in later years and especially so when I was writing this book. Indeed without the help of these old diaries I would probably not have attempted it.

We always had the benefit of a plentiful supply of fibrous loam, the source of which was situated adjacent to the gardens. It was cut from a wide open lane which served as a bridle road from Aynhoe to King's Sutton, the next village. The turves were about four inches thick and laid on a bed of loose sand stone and consequently they were a mass of fibre. We maintained two separate stacks of turves, and as soon as one of them was expended, another supply was cut and stacked. Loam was of course the foundation of almost all the potting mixtures and the second most important ingredient was leaf soil, a commodity which was plentiful and was gathered from a private road which ran through the Estate between avenues of beech and oak trees. Several heaps of this leaf soil were maintained, all of different maturity.

One of my tasks during the early winter months was to ensure that there were plentiful supplies of loam and leaf soil ready for use in the annexe to the potting shed, thus enabling potting up to continue regardless of the weather prevailing at the time. Peat was used only for the rarer plants such as orchids, ferns, and azaleas. We used a similar ingredient for rooting cuttings. It was called coconut refuse, and a four bushel bag could be purchased for only 3/9d. Silver sand was incorporated in the more important composts, whilst for use in the less important mixtures we were able to obtain supplies of sharp sand from our own pits. To-day however I use ordinary gravel after the very fine sand has been sifted out. The size of the particles used depends upon the size and type of plant to be potted. We also stored old lime mortar rubble obtained from the old walls and cottages on the Estate. The lime used on the vegetable plots and for lime-washing the walls of the greenhouses was bought from a lime kiln.

I wonder how many people recognise the value of soot in the garden, and indeed I cannot stress its value too highly. It is a valuable fertiliser in the vegetable garden and on the lawns, and is extremely effective wherever slugs are troublesome. We had a contract with the local sweep at Aynhoe and purchased all the soot he could provide. Sometimes we kept as many as three heaps with more than a ton in each heap, and we never used the soot until it had been allowed to stand for at least twelve months. All the soot from the Park House chimneys was stored and eventually mixed with leaf soil as a top dressing for the lawns, which was applied in the early part of the spring, one bucket of soot to one barrow load of leaf soil passed through a half inch sieve. In the autumn the lawns were again top dressed with leaf soil, but when this was done basic slag was added instead of soot, a much smaller amount being required in proportion to the leaf soil.

It was at this time of my gardening career that a number of my friends and I who had not quite reached military age enlisted in the Volunteers, a similar organisation to the Home Guard formed during the Second World War. Initially we were not considered old enough to carry arms, and so we were formed into a bugle band and very proudly marched at the head of our local platoon. By the time the war ended in November I was trained in the use of the rifle and bayonet, and in handling a grenade. A week after the Armistice was signed I would have been seventeen years of age, and liable to be called upon to join the regular army for home defence. In fact I did receive my calling up papers, but I was not required to enlist. If I had of course my unbroken service in the gardens at Aynhoe would have been interrupted, and who knows whether I would have returned there.

CHAPTER TEN
An Orchid Called Portia

ONE SATURDAY AFTERNOON DURING THE EARLY twenties, I was summoned to the Grammar House by my employers, who handed me two plants of *Cattleya portia* in bloom, which they had just purchased from Harrods of London.

The orchids were growing in eight-inch pots, or so it appeared to me at the time. Later however, I realised that they had merely been pushed into the pots, having been imported by the London store.

At that time my knowledge of orchids was limited, and one of the plants soon began to look rather sick, and finally it died. The head gardener, whose experience of orchids was no wider than mine, expressed the opinion that the remaining plant would also die very shortly, and he was quite content to entrust me with the care of the survivor. Little did I realise then that this plant was destined to become world famous, and would be seen by millions on the television screen.

For a number of years I grew the plant in a mixture of coarse peat and sphagnum moss, a little charcoal and coarse silver sand, and it was not until the plant was growing in a twelve-inch pot and carrying about sixty blooms that I was first introduced to osmunda fibre. An orchid grower who was interested in my cattleya told me about this most important compost ingredient, and also instructed me in its preparation, and assisted me to re-pot the plant. I have always felt indebted to this man for his timely tuition. He has been dead for a number of years now, but I often think how pleased he would be with the fine specimen this plant has become.

The cattleya grew stronger in its new preparation, and it became necessary to divide it into three, and it was soon noticeable that one plant was growing rapidly ahead of the other two. Eventually all three plants were accommodated in separate twelve-inch pots, and in November 1938 I was persuaded to exhibit them at the Royal Horticultural Society Show at Westminster. Between them the plants carried a total of a hundred and ninety perfect soft mauve blooms and they were awarded the Lindley Medal.

Amongst the many congratulatory letters I received was the following tribute from Mr. H. H. Alexandra, V.M.H., a man whose name must be known to every orchid grower in the world, and who was for many years a member of the Orchid Committee of the Royal Horticultural Society.

> *I am delighted to read of your achievement in winning the Lindley Medal, with your magnificent* Cattleya portia. *This is indeed something of which to be proud, for this high award is rarely given and I am sure your plants must have caused a sensation.*

Another letter which gave me pleasure was one which I received from Mr. Wood of William Wood & Sons Ltd., of Taplow, Bucks.

> *Will you please accept my very hearty congratulations on your three pots of* Cattleya portia, *and the award you were given,*

which was most highly deserved. I was walking down the hall before I had been up to see the plants put up for an award, and met the Hon. Mr. Tufton, whom as you know is an enthusiastic orchid grower. He said to me 'Have you seen the wonderful orchids at the end of the hall'.

Several weeks after this memorable occasion I was browsing through a gardening journal when I came across a picture of *Cattleya trianae*, variety *hydra*, which boasted ninety-six blooms, and had been grown by Mr. Alexandra himself. This was the incentive I needed, and I was determined to produce a single cattleya which would carry over a hundred blooms. This ambition was realised sooner than I imagined for the following year the larger plant, which had persisted in keeping ahead of the other two, produced one hundred and thirty-nine blooms.

I was assured by the secretary of the Royal Horticultural Society that there was no record of any other single cattleya ever having borne this number of blooms. During the cultivation of these specimen plants I had a number of spikes each with ten blooms. This however was not a record, for a spike shown by Messrs. Charlesworth and Co. in 1914 carried sixteen blooms.

The greenhouse which has been the home of the *Cattleya portia* for forty years is an old lean-to vinery constructed of Russian pine, and has stood for over two hundred years. The back wall is fifteen feet high, it is thirty feet in length, and fifteen feet wide, and incidentally, this is the same house from which I cut out the vine rods in 1917.

During the cattleya's lifetime at Aynhoe, we have on more than one occasion been faced with a crisis with regards to its welfare, and it is on reflection very fortunate that the plant is alive and flourishing to-day. From 1940 onwards the war meant a turnover to food production, and therefore less time could be allocated to orchid culture. During the winter of 1941, the hot water system in the greenhouse failed as a result of a burst pipe in the chimney stack near the boiler. Two long nights passed before this set-back could be rectified, and in the meantime emergency heating facilities were implemented. These consisted of an electric fire and two paraffin lamps, which were placed in empty water barrels. Sheets of tin were placed about one foot above each container and served to conserve the heat, and also subdue the light. By this method the night temperature was maintained at just above freezing level.

The plants were in flower at the time, and the fall in temperature caused by this inopportune break-down resulted in the majority of the blooms becoming chilled and collapsing in consequence. Many of the leading growths turned black, especially those nearest the glass.

The obvious solution would have been to have moved the plants to an adjacent smaller greenhouse, but unfortunately the other houses were not equipped with power points, and furthermore the task of moving the plant, which had by then attained mammoth proportions, by myself, was impossible. The only help I had during the war years was that of a young girl, the rest of the staff having either been enlisted for military service or directed to other war work.

Having installed the electric fire and paraffin heaters as temporary measures, I was faced with an additional problem —the blackout regulations. The greenhouses were situated in the centre of a military camp used for storing petrol and oil, and consequently it was imperative that not one chink of light should be visible from the air. Locating and fixing blinds over the house before darkness fell was a difficult task, but it was successfully completed minutes before the deadline.

My emergency methods were mercifully sufficient to pull the plants through, and in 1942, the largest plant, which was growing in a twenty-one-inch pan fourteen inches deep, produced twenty-two spikes bearing one hundred and forty-two blooms. The second plant carried one hundred and three blooms and the remaining plant which I had been forced to divide in two following the damage sustained during the 1941 winter, produced forty-six and thirty-six blooms respectively. During the spring of 1943 I re-potted these two plants, and transferred the largest plant into a hexagonal shaped box about thirty inches in diameter and fifteen inches deep.

During the remainder of the war years, the plants did not receive all the attention they required, but nevertheless I devoted whatever spare time I could find to their care, and they continued to flourish, until in 1947 the three plants produced eighty spikes, bearing a total of five hundred and five blooms.

In the spring of 1948, exactly ten years after originally showing the plants in London, I decided to present them for a second time, and having made this decision, I was faced with a fresh problem, one of transportation. I realised that when the plants were in bloom it would be impossible to move them through the greenhouse door without damaging the flowers, and therefore I decided to transfer the plants whilst they were still in the resting stage into an adjacent lean-to vinery, and in order to put this operation into effect it became necessary to tie the leaves of the plants tightly together. In this way we were able to squeeze the plants through the greenhouse doorway without damaging them.

The construction of the vinery, which was to become the orchids' new quarters, was such that it suited my plans for the removal of the plants at show time admirably, inasmuch as the main rafters of the roof were four feet apart, and between each rafter were two lights which could easily be unscrewed and removed. It would then be a fairly simple operation with sufficient help to lift the plants out when the time came.

Whilst transferring the plants into their new quarters, my plans were almost thwarted when the wooden container in which one of the plants rested collapsed as it was being manoeuvred through the greenhouse door. I hurriedly constructed another wooden container, and gradually eased the fallen plant into it, carefully re-planting it as I did so, and hopefully I took it to join its companions. I was relieved during the ensuing weeks to notice that it appeared to be none the worse for the shaking up it had received.

A week prior to the R.H.S. Show, I constructed three

plant carriers, each a little larger than the boxes in which the cattleyas were growing. On Sunday November 28th, having recruited some extra help, I removed the plants from the lean-to vinery, and transferred them to an outhouse which was adjacent to the main road. Paraffin lamps were placed in the building overnight to provide heat for the orchids, and early the following morning they were loaded into a furniture removal van, and then began what for me was to be a nightmare journey.

During the whole of the seventy mile trek to London, I was imprisoned in the rear of the van, in almost total darkness, with my precious plants. The weather conditions could not have been worse, the driver had to contend with freezing fog, and the roads were treacherous because of ice. On several occasions I felt the vehicle skidding, and in the circumstances it was indeed fortunate that I had decided to suffer the ordeal of travelling in the rear with the orchids, for I was often able to steady the plants when they would otherwise have slid or keeled over and sustained serious damage and bruising to the blooms. The journey, accompanied as it was by sudden bumps and emergency stops, seemed to be endless, for of course I did not have the faintest idea of our position, but finally the van came to a grinding halt, and the driver came round to the rear and informed me we were outside the R.H.S. Hall at last.

Inside the Society's Headquarters, a long low table was put at my disposal, and I arranged the three plants along its length, placing the largest orchid in the centre. Between the plants I placed several large pots of fern and around the base of the whole exhibit, I built up a bed of moss supported on wire mesh, and around the table I trailed the fern *Asparagus sprengeri*. The mass of luxurious mauve blooms emerging from this large expanse of greenery was most effective, and on the Tuesday morning I reaped my reward, the Lindley Silver Medal, and I felt that all the time and trouble and setbacks I had experienced during the foregoing months had been more than worthwhile. The three plants carried a total of five hundred and twenty-six blooms.

John Lindley, after whom the medal was named, died on November 1st 1865. The Council of the Horticultural Society, learning that his library was coming up for sale, resolved to purchase it, and now a hundred years later, greatly enriched and added to, it forms the nucleus at Vincent Square of one of the greatest, if not the greatest, horticultural libraries in the world. The Council further determined to commemorate him by the institution of a Lindley medal, and the recipients of the first award were Messrs. Veitch of Chelsea in December 1865. It is now considered to be one of the Society's most esteemed awards, and it is given for an exhibit of a plant or plants of special interest or beauty, or an exhibit displaying exceptional skill in cultivation or for educational exhibits.

By 1950 the total had increased to six hundred and nineteen blooms, the majority of which were despatched to Messrs. Geo. Monro Ltd., Covent Market, and realised just over £100.

In 1952, I wrote a brief history of the plants for the readers of the *Australian Orchid Review*, and in his letter of thanks the editor wrote that whilst many of his country's native orchids made wonderful specimen plants, the blooms were small in comparison to *Cattleya portia*, and he knew of no exotic variety to compare with the remarkable specimens at Aynhoe.

In November 1952 the plants were featured in the B.B.C. sound programme *What Goes on*, when I was interviewed by Mr. Bill Hartley, and as a result of this broadcast the orchids became known to a wider range of interested horticulturists, and I found that I was required to answer a considerable amount of correspondence as a result.

By November 1954, the largest plant, which by this time measured six feet across, produced fifty spikes, bearing three hundred and twenty-two blooms, the second plant forty-seven spikes, bearing two hundred and eighty-six blooms, and the third plant produced one hundred and sixty-three blooms, making a grand total of seven hundred and seventy-one blooms. In that same year the December issue of the American Orchid Society's *Bulletin* published an article by Dr. Ella Grey of California, entitled *Portias at Christmas*. Mention of my plants was made, and paved the way for correspondence between Dr. Grey and myself. This correspondence was to prove most beneficial from my viewpoint, particularly with regard to the culture of the portias.

For a number of years, Dr. Grey experimented with the control of the flowering period of *Cattleya portia*, and had demonstrated that the flowering of most *labiata* hybrids could be controlled by light.

Cattleya portia normally blooms during the month of November and is a suitable subject for controlled flowering because the blooms on the various spikes open at about the same time, therefore by prolonging the hours of daylight their flowering can be delayed until Christmas. As we are all aware, after June 21st, the longest day, the hours of daylight gradually lessen. Therefore to achieve our objective, artificial lights controlled by a time clock must be introduced during the last week of June. These lights according to Dr. Grey should be switched on at dusk, and continue burning for four hours. Later on in the year, during autumn, they should be allowed to burn for five hours each night. This system ensures that the plants receive approximately sixteen hours of light each day. Incandescent 100 watt lamps should be used, and these can be placed at intervals of ten feet and ideally should be suspended about three feet above the plants. During the middle of October the lights should cease to be used and the plants should be allowed to continue normally.

Obviously this system can be varied slightly to suit particular plants and conditions, and indeed when I first instituted Dr. Grey's methods at Aynhoe, I did not meet with complete success. I carried out the light experiment exactly as Dr. Grey advised during 1956, but the flowering was delayed too long, and as a result a small number of blooms were ready for Christmas, but the majority did not flower until January. The following year I dispensed with the lights on the assumption that as the orchids had flowered a month in arrears during the previous year, they would automatically be retarded, and next time round they would flower in December. However, this assumption proved to be incorrect, for they flowered at their normal time in November.

The next year I varied Dr. Grey's original recipe, and from the end of June I used the lights for three hours only each night until mid-October, and this had the required effect, for the plants commenced to bloom during the early part of December, with the result that the flowers were in perfect condition for the Christmas market.

The orchids, which were frequently mentioned in various gardening journals, continually aroused interest in many parts of the world, and amongst the articles which I wrote in connection with the plants was one published in the December 1955 issue of the American Orchid Society journal, following which I received a letter from the editor saying that he knew of no specimen cattleya in that country to equal mine.

In 1959 the plants produced more spikes than hitherto, and a fine mass of blooms was expected. Mr. Paul Morby the producer of the B.B.C. Television programme *Gardening Club*, showed an interest in the plants, and during the month of October he called at Aynhoe to see the orchids. As a result of his visit, he decided that the plants should be televised when they were in bloom, and to my surprise he also invited me to appear with Percy Thrower on *Gardening Club* at the same time. Frankly, the idea terrified me, and it was something for which I was totally unprepared. However, Mr. Morby did not press me to accept straightaway, but he invited me to attend the Birmingham Television Studios in order that I might study at first hand how a television programme is produced. I visited the studios shortly after Mr. Morby's visit, and although I was overawed at the vast preparation which is necessary before a programme is televised, some of my fears were allayed, and I agreed to take the plunge.

The orchids were filmed in the greenhouse at Aynhoe on December 1st, and they really looked their best carrying over eight hundred blooms. At the same time, cameramen from a nearby U.S. base took the opportunity of filming the orchids, and as a result of their interest, the Aynhoe plants are mentioned in the American Cooks Tours brochures of European Holidays, as being well worth a visit.

So it was that at 11 a.m. on 14th January 1960, I arrived with some trepidation at the Birmingham Television Studios. I had taken with me a number of plants, chiefly orchids, as part of the programme was scheduled to be shown live, and part was to be devoted to the film taken earlier at Aynhoe. It will no doubt be of interest to the reader to learn of the preparation and presentation of *Gardening Club*, and therefore I will try to describe my impressions of my first television appearance.

On arrival at the studio I found the carpenters busily engaged in erecting a garden shed, which was minus one side piece in order that the cameras would be able to intrude. They had already erected the well known *Gardening Club* greenhouse, which for obvious technical reasons has no glass. This was put at my disposal and I began to arrange the plants I had brought with me on the staging inside. The remainder of the morning I spent in discussion with Paul Morby and Percy Thrower, whilst a secretary made notes of the points raised. Both Paul Morby and Percy Thrower are perfectionists, and they spare no pains to ensure that there will be no last minute hitches when the show is ready to go on.

At 2 p.m. the cameramen and technicians arrive on the studio floor. Three cameras are used, mounted on their dollies so that they can be completely mobile under the directions of the skilful technicians in charge of them. The producer, high up in his box above the studio floor, has before him three screens on to which are projected the images being filmed by the three cameras in use, and he decides which picture reaches the viewers' homes. During the time the programme is being screened the producer is able to speak to his cameramen by telephone, and direct them as necessary. The floor manager, also connected by telephone, is on the spot to interpret the producer's directions.

During the afternoon whilst the programme was being rehearsed, I began to get butterflies in my stomach. The problems of presenting an unscripted programme to millions of viewers by 6.10 p.m. that evening seemed to me to be insurmountable, particularly bearing in mind that the producer and Percy Thrower had to contend with an inexperienced and nervous guest, for that is how I felt. I need not have been so concerned, for both Paul Morby and Percy Thrower had dealt with nervous guests before, and had become past masters in the art of piecing together a programme, and knowing just how long to allot for each item. The outward calm and friendly manner which has made Percy Thrower one of the most popular personalities on television is all the more remarkable when one stops to consider the numerous problems with which he must concern himself during the transmission of *Gardening Club*. He must foster and guide an intelligent conversation throughout the programme without the aid of a script. He must ensure that the sequence followed during rehearsals is adhered to during the actual programme. He must constantly keep one eye on the clock, and watch the monitor sets at the same time to ensure that the dialogue coincides with the picture being screened. He must ensure that the programme content is intelligible to the viewer, and with all these things on his mind, he must appear to be perfectly relaxed and at ease.

Once the programme had got under way and I had been introduced by Percy, I forgot my nervousness, and became engrossed in the matter at hand, which after all revolved around subjects with which I had been conversant for most of my life. At the conclusion of the programme, Paul Morby and Percy assured me that it had been a success, and I for my part suddenly realised what a major part Percy plays in the programme, with his casual prompting, and his easy affable manner which radiates confidence in other participants in the programme, particularly if they are newcomers like myself.

I realised what a wide audience the programme commands when during the ensuing weeks I received over a hundred letters from viewers, saying that they had enjoyed the programme, and many of them requesting further information on the cultivation of orchids. Many more letters were forwarded direct to the B.B.C., some of which were passed on to me by Mr. Morby in order that I might reply to them.

It may or may not be significant, that the majority of letters I received were written by the fairer sex. I believe that this may be due to the fact that because of the materials used in their cultivation, orchid growing is a relatively clean hobby. Of all the correspondence which I received at that time, and many of the letters were from quite eminent people, one in particular I found very touching. It was written by an old lady of seventy-eight years who lived alone in a small cottage near Bletchley in Buckinghamshire. I have retained her letter, and I consider it is worthy of mention here. She wrote:—

Dear Sir,

I am writing to ask you if you would do me a great favour. I am 78 years old, and I have got arthritis very bad and cannot get about. I saw you on the B.B.C. with Mr. Thrower last Friday when you showed us some lovely orchids which you had, which I enjoyed very much. I think they were lovely.

I have one which you speak about, a white one with yellow in the centre, and which wants re-potting. I wondered if you could get me a bag of the potting mixture which you showed us on T.V. and send it to me as I can't get out to the shops, and don't know what to ask for. I couldn't catch the name of the mixture, and if you would like me to send the money first, if you would let me I would send the money on to you.

An old lady next door gave it to me before she died 2 years ago. It had ten blooms then, and someone told me to re-pot it as it wanted it. I done it and it has not done so well since, but it had only earth soil, not like the mixture you showed us. I see it has three blooms coming on it now, and could you please tell me when it is right to re-pot it.

I am very fond of flowers and enjoyed your orchids you showed us very much. I only wished I had the money and could afford to buy some of your orchids. As I saw in the programme you were sending some orchids to Covent Garden, but I only get my pension and cannot afford to buy them. If you could let me know, if you can kindly do this for me, I should be very grateful. I am sorry to ask you.

I remain yours truly
(A. Andrews)

P.S. I have a large bowl made the same as a flower pot which is 10 inches, and four inches deep, will that do to transplant the orchid in?

Needless to say I replied to this letter, advising the old lady as to the best method of re-potting her precious orchid, and informing her that I had forwarded to her free of charge a mixture of the orchid compost identical to that she had seen me prepare on T.V. She has since written to express her gratitude and tells me her plant is thriving.

Another most interesting letter which I received at this time enlightened me as to the origin of *Cattleya portia*. Mr. Robert Tunstill of the Old Manor House, Bradford-on-Avon, Wiltshire, wrote to say that an account of the Portia which he had just read in a copy of the *Banbury Advertiser* had interested him greatly because his father Robert Turnstill had raised the original plant in his orchid houses at Monkholme, Brierfield, near Burnley. He went on to say that his father, who was part owner of a large cotton mill, died in 1903, whereupon his mother gave up the cultivation of orchids, and the houses fell into disuse.

December 1962 brought the usual lovely display of blooms, but low temperatures brought about by the severe weather which set in during late December that year and carried on into mid-February affected the plants and caused grave concern. Indeed, the winter of 1962/63 was the worst in living memory.

The house in which the cattleyas were growing at that time was heated with Humex electrical heaters, and a small hard fuel boiler which supplied heat to sixty feet of four-inch pipes. This heating system was sufficient to maintain a temperature of 60 to 65 degrees Fahrenheit through a normal winter. During these critical months however, although the hard fuel boiler was sustained at top pressure both day and night, very little heat was radiated by the electric heaters owing to frequent power cuts, with the result that the temperature during the whole of January, and the beginning of February, even allowing for some heat from the sun, rarely exceeded 50 degrees Fahrenheit.

On two nights, when the outside temperature dropped to below zero, the house temperature was only 40 degrees Fahrenheit, and ice formed on the inside of the glass. Most mornings the temperature read between 45 and 48 degrees Fahrenheit. As is often the case, it never rains but it pours, and I was taken ill in the midst of this crisis, and was compelled to stay away from work, the first time for over twenty years. I was obliged to rely upon the good services of a young man who had been my assistant for only a few months, and whose knowledge of the plants was negligible; a retired railwayman who had previously helped me out in the garden on numerous occasions; and a former employee. He volunteered to look after the hard fuel boiler during the hours of darkness, and in this time of need he proved to be a friend indeed.

I left instructions that no plant should receive water unless it showed signs of distress, and that the house was to be kept as dry as possible. Any water which might be spilt, or which might fall from the roof, was to be mopped up. As the severe spell of weather began to subside, I was able to return to work, and anxiously I inspected my precious charges. As I had feared, most of the growths were in a distressed condition, although there were some which appeared to have suffered little damage. I decided there and then that something had to be done if I was to salvage the orchids. For some time, I had toyed with the idea of planting the three plants together in one container, and so I decided that this would be as good a time as any to try it.

I secured a number of one-inch boards, each five inches in width, and after treating them with cuprinol, I bored several holes in each piece in order to admit air into the box I planned to make. The box would have to be built around the three plants as they stood, and in three stages, one board high at each stage, and the orchids would be re-planted as I progressed. The container was to be fourteen feet in length and five feet wide at the base, increasing to fifteen feet long and six feet wide at the top, and it would be bottomless. I began to prepare the necessary compost in different grades from my stock of osmunda fibre and sphagnum moss. Drainage materials also had to be thought of.

I commenced the operation towards the end of March, and my first task was to break away the almost rotten wooden containers which had hitherto held the plants. I placed the bottom layer of boards into position, and filled the spaces left with drainage material. Then, taking great care not to damage any of the live roots, I very meticulously removed the spent compost and decayed roots, and replaced it with the new mixture. The whole operation took three days, and it soon became apparent that the orchids had weathered the storm and were flourishing once again.

The following December I harvested four hundred blooms, many of which realised five shillings each in Covent Garden market. From the proceeds I was able to invest in a new five-sectional hard fuel boiler to supplement the existing heating system. This meant that a further four hundred feet of four-inch pipes were able to be utilised, and much to my surprise, although they had not been in use for ten years, they functioned perfectly and no leaks appeared. With this additional aid to the heating system, and the electric heaters thermostatically controlled so that they automatically take over when temperature drops sharply, I now have no worries about maintaining the correct temperature, whatever the weather.

In 1964 the plant yielded over five hundred and fifty blooms, and in addition a number of young growths appeared, and these will produce blooms within the next two years. In 1965 over six hundred blooms were yielded and in 1967 six hundred and twenty-nine blooms.

One problem which has always faced me has been the relatively short period of about four weeks during which the blooms come and go. This means of course that all the flowers have to be sold in a short space of time, and it is more difficult to obtain a good market price for them. To overcome this problem I decided to extend the flowering period, and this I was able to do by prolonging the length of light over one part of the plant only. By using this method I was able to double the normal flowering period.

The *Cattleya portia* has been in my care now for over forty years, and not unnaturally I have become very attached to it, and indeed it has become part of my life. I have two ambitions left in respect of this plant, namely that it will eventually bear a thousand blooms, and that its true beauty will be transmitted to all horticulturists by means of colour television.

CHAPTER ELEVEN

Gardening Through the 1920's

A T LAST THE LONG STRUGGLE OF WAR ENDED
with the signing of the Armistice, and some of the
labour began to return, but as in every hamlet and
town through the land some did not return, and we were so
much poorer because of an unmarked grave in a distant
land.

In the spring of 1919 the foreman gardener decided to
leave. This left Mr. Brown and myself together with a young
lad from the village to carry on as best we could until a
suitable replacement could be found. It was not until the
early autumn that Mr. Brown was able to engage another
foreman. This man who came from Sir Ernest Cassel's
gardens was an exceptionally skilled gardener, especially
under glass, and being a single man, after a short while he
wanted me to share his quarters. I accepted and so began my
second spell in the bothy. During the next twelve months
I was required to accept far more responsibility than hitherto.

I learnt quickly during this time and easily remembered what I was taught, not having on my mind the host of teenage problems that beset the boys of to-day. I got on extremely well with my new foreman, who was a confirmed bachelor, and he was able to devote a great deal of his spare time to assisting me with my studies.

During the late autumn of 1920, for reasons which were not divulged, there was a reduction in expenditure throughout the Estate. However no one who had worked on the Estate for any length of time was dismissed. Such employees were however restricted to a few days work each week, but to compensate them, and to help them over any financial worries caused by these economic measures, they were allowed to work for themselves on two days each week cutting down dead trees, and lopping off the lower boughs of other trees along nearly two miles of the main road. This wood when brought into the timber yard and sawn into logs realised for the men far more money than they lost in wages through short time. The garden staff were not so fortunate, Two men were required to leave, one from the kitchen garden and one from the pleasure grounds. The bothy was closed and consequently the foreman also left and so at the age of nineteen I was asked to take charge of the greenhouses and house decoration with only a boy to help me. I agreed to do this on condition I was given a free hand, and Mr. Brown accepted my condition but reserved the right to correct me if I failed to give satisfaction. I was confident on this score, and this was not conceit, but most certainly due in no small way to the excellent tuition I had received from two expert plantsman.

I was allowed to retain the heat in the four vineries and the two stove houses, but all the others including the peach houses now became unheated. My first task was to decide on the most suitable plants for the house. Naturally this selection included the few orchids which we grew, then those others no longer required, including the palms, were burnt. Violets were limited to one frame only. Sadly I was obliged to cut the vines out of three vineries, keeping only the muscats. One house nearest the boiler was adapted as a stove house with a minimum night temperature of 60 degrees Fahrenheit. The little stove house with its separate boiler I decided to heat for only three months, namely February, March and April. I realised that this was a great sacrifice, for the little stove was an ideal house, where all our seeds were raised, and our cuttings propagated. I failed to see how I was to overcome this liability until one day, whilst watering plants on the back wall shelves in the vineries, the rose fell from my watering can into the hot water pipe channel which ran through the house to the other vineries. Whilst retrieving the rose I suddenly realised that here with a little improvisation was a place that would make an ideal propagating frame. Using a trowel I removed the soil that partly covered the return pipe. I then placed a half-inch wire mesh over the pipes and covered the wire with a thick layer of moss which I had previously sterilised with boiling water. On top of the moss I laid a three-inch layer of coconut fibre. I then constructed a frame to fit over the channel, the glass of which sloped at the same angle as the vinery roof. The wood work and all surrounding areas were painted white to reflect as much light as possible into the frame. On a previous occasion I had noticed somewhere a large mirror fixed to a wall so as to reflect light into a cellar, and so I also implemented this idea into my scheme. One day whilst working in the vineries Mr. Brown passed through with an old gardening friend. The old gentleman paused for a while before enquiring of Mr. Brown whose idea was the propagating frame. When Mr. Brown informed him that I was responsible, the old man remarked, 'You won't have to worry about him if he has ideas like that'. These few words encouraged me enormously as praise was very sparingly given in those days. If you could not do your job, you quickly made room for someone else.

The restraint on expenditure was gradually released and eventually I was able to engage another village boy and in 1922 we were able to use heat again in the two larger plant houses. With only the smaller Grammar House to supply with produce we did not engage any more staff either in the kitchen garden or the pleasure grounds. We might well have done so for at this stage the young squire and his former tutor who had subsequently taken over the management of the Estate decided to transform large areas which had hitherto been covered with evergreens such as laurel. Many large elm trees, some as high as a hundred and twenty feet, were felled, and large shrubs such as hollies and laurels were uprooted from the north side of the Park House leaving it completely open to the main road for the first time, thus affording motorists passing through the village a fine view of the house. About half way between the house and road a low curved wall was built along the entire frontage, two openings being left to accommodate the driveways. The trees and shrubs were replaced by lawns and a series of beds which were planted with polyanthus roses. A large bed in the shape of a half circle was laid inside the curved wall. This bed accommodated up to five hundred bedding plants and it became my responsibility to provide them. Several acres of evergreens situated between the Park House and the kitchen garden were also grubbed out together with some of the forest trees there. The whole area was sown with grass seed, after which thousands of bulbs were planted, daffodils, narcissi, crocuses, snowdrops, scillas, grape hyacinths and bluebells. Thereafter every spring the pleasure grounds were transformed into a panorama of colour. Daffodil Sunday was innovated at Aynhoe when the grounds were opened to the public, and a band was engaged to play light music during the afternoon.

My chief task during this time was to supply plants and cut flowers for the house, but having a free hand I began to experiment in the cultivation of the rarer type of plants including orchids. I also formed a keen interest in the cultivation of peaches and nectarines and was to derive great pleasure in growing these fruits during the ensuing years. More beds began to appear in the pleasure grounds and I was kept busy providing an increasing number of bedding plants to fill them.

During the next few years I continued to specialise in various kinds of pot plants for house decoration, amongst which were azaleas, pelargoniums, calceolarias, cinerarias, cyclamen, fibrous-rooted begonias, and bulbs such as hippeastrums, achimenes, gloxinias, and gesneras or smithianthas as they are now known.

I always found the task of raising cyclamen to be a very rewarding one, probably because they flower over such a long period during winter and spring. The prolonged flowering period is made possible by sowing at regular intervals from May until August. The greenhouse variety *Cyclamen persicum* evolved from the Persian cyclamen which grows wild in Greece, Palestine and parts of Syria. It is a cool house plant, and needs a temperature of around 50 degrees Fahrenheit.

Cyclamen are extremely popular, many thousands being sold annually, particularly at Christmas time, and therefore raising them from seed can become a profitable hobby. The seed should be obtained from a reputable firm, bearing in mind that no extra time or space is required in growing a good strain than there is in growing a poor variety, but the final results are vastly different.

Prior to sowing the seed, pans should be soaked; then you prepare the seed bed from a John Innes compost, adding a sprinkling of fine silver sand. Small holes the depth of the seed should be made about one inch apart. I always find a pencil is the most suitable tool for this operation. Having placed a single seed in each hole, they should be covered with another sprinkling of fine silver sand, followed by a fine layer of soil. The pan can then be placed in the greenhouse and covered over with a slate.

The slate remains in position until the seedlings begin to appear, and then it is removed and the pan should be placed on a shelf near the roof glass so as to prevent the seedlings from becoming drawn; at the same time however, care should be taken not to expose them to the hot sun. Thus the seedlings remain until they become strong enough to be potted singly into two and a half-inch pots. Once again a

John Innes compost can be used. It is the normal practice to pot the corms so that they are half in and half out of the soil. However, I prefer to place the corm just below the surface for the initial potting because I find that a light covering of compost over the corms keeps the skin softer and thereby induces better leaf production. Thereafter the plants are re-potted until they are fully grown, and on these occasions I no longer fully cover the corm. This operation of transferring the plant in stages from one pot to another is often referred to as Take & Pot.

The cyclamen must have an open soil, and indeed it will never do well without it. Furthermore it welcomes the presence of lime, and the addition of crushed mortar rubble in its compost is essential.

Crushed chalk or ground limestone is generally used to-day. Modern mortar comprises a double hydrate silicate of calcium and alimina, and possesses much more durable qualities, but because it is made from Portland cement and not lime mortar, the lime it contains is no more available to plants than potash is in broken glass. All my life when potting cyclamen and other lime loving plants I have used old mortar rubble. My supply to-day comes from one-inch plaster taken from the walls inside the old potting shed which was once the old bothy. As the plant reaches its maturity it should be kept in a light airy position under glass. This prevents it becoming drawn and weak. It should be watered liberally when growth is free and active, and shaded during hot sunny spells of weather. Dewing over several times a day with tepid rain water will encourage clean healthy growth, but as soon as the flower buds begin to show above the foliage, overhead damping must cease, and be confined to the area immediately surrounding the plant.

By removing the old flowers as soon as they begin to fade, it is possible to prolong the flowering period considerably. When the blooms have finally disappeared, the application of water should gradually be withheld, and thus the tubers are able to dry off. During the summer the plants can be placed in a cold frame and covered over with peat or leaf soil so that the tubers remain about half an inch below the surface. In this state they should be watered occasionally during dry spells, although the seasonal rainfall is usually sufficient. The new growth will easily break through, and as soon as the top dressing begins to rise, the plants can be lifted and very carefully removed from their pots. After most of the soil has been removed from the plant, care being taken not to damage the live roots, the cyclamen can be re-potted in fresh compost, and thereafter its treatment follows the same pattern as for young plants.

Anyone who is fortunate enough to have a cyclamen in his home would do well to remember that it should be kept in a light place, and be free from draughts. It is an advantage if the plant is stood in a container which has about an inch of gravel, and water to the depth of three quarters of an inch in the bottom. The plant should always be allowed to dry out even to the point of flagging, whereupon it should be placed in a bowl of water, the level of which is a little higher than the soil level. After it has remained in water for an hour or more it will have become thoroughly soaked, and it may then be removed, and will require no more water until once more it shows signs of flagging.

July 1924 saw the coming of age of Richard, the only son of Sir Fairfax and Lady Cartwright. This was indeed an auspicious occasion, and was to be celebrated in a lavish and extravagant manner typical of those times.

During the spring of that year, we in the gardens were making special preparations to ensure that there would be adequate floral displays in the pleasure grounds, and additional pot plants available to decorate the Park House during the ensuing celebrations. To overcome the problem of space in the greenhouses, and to make way for additional plants, we transferred a thousand geraniums in pots from the greenhouses to the vacant celery trenches in the adjoining kitchen garden. This operation took place in April, and so as to prevent the plants from being damaged and blown over by the wind, quantities of leaf soil were placed around and between the pots. At night time the plants were further protected by cloches and this procedure ensured that they were in bloom and properly hardened off by the time we needed them.

The coming of age celebrations were to last for eight days, and were attended by hundreds of guests, many of whom were visitors from abroad. An enormous marquee had been erected on the lawn near the Park House, and it was here that the guests dined during their stay. It was my duty to provide fresh flowers for the tables each morning both in the marquee and in the Park House. On the actual birthday, I decorated the dinner table with an arrangement of rambler roses picked from the Rose Garden. This simple idea was most effective and received generous praise.

The celebrations concluded with a mammoth firework display which took place at the front of the Park House. The event was witnessed by thousands of sightseers who had thought it worthwhile to travel several miles from the surrounding countryside.

There was at this time, and there still is, a ha-ha which separates the lawn at the front of the house from the park-land beyond. This construction, which is not uncommon on estates in this country, consists of a wall which is sunk where the pleasure gardens meet the park land, and is inconspicuous from the house and gardens. There is a ditch on the park land side of the wall and the purpose of the ha-ha is to prevent the cattle and deer from intruding into the pleasure grounds. A further advantage of this type of boundary is that it affords uninterrupted views of the surrounding countryside. The ha-ha at Aynhoe is four hundred and sixty yards in length, and varies from between seven and eight feet in depth. On the park side the ditch opens out become a sloping bank, which at its crest is slightly lower than the level of the lawn, thus corresponding with the surrounding park land which slopes gently away from the house and grounds. In spite of the very considerable protection that the ha-ha provides, during severe winters, when snow has lain on the ground, I have known deer in search of food to leap across the ha-ha on to the lawns, with the result that young trees, shrubs, and rose bushes have sustained serious damage.

During the firework display which I have described, one of the spectators, striving to reach a more advantageous position from which to observe the proceedings, disappeared over the edge of the ha-ha, the presence of which she had been totally unaware of, and as a result of her fall the unhappy lady sustained a broken leg.

Another story often recounted by the older villagers illustrates how well the presence of the ha-ha is camouflaged. Apparently, during the First World War, a regular army sergeant was drilling a squad of local territorials on the lawn in front of the Park House. Instead of bringing the party to a halt at the edge of the lawn, and standing them at ease, he turned for a few seconds to admire the architecture of the House. On turning round to resume drill instruction, he discovered that he no longer had anyone to drill. It seemed to the mystified sergeant that his men had been

spirited away by some unseen force, but had he known of the presence of the ha-ha he would have quickly assessed the situation.

In the spring of 1925 I asked Mr. Brown if the bothy could be reopened, as I intended to marry and would like to make it my home. Sir Fairfax and Lady Cartwright gave their consent and immediately the carpenters and decorators were called in, and the bothy was quickly transformed into a very pleasant home. And so on the 21st day of April I was married and took up residence in the bothy for the third time.

CHAPTER TWELVE

Head Gardener

IN 1928 SIR FAIRFAX CARTWRIGHT DIED, AND SO
only four years after having come of age Richard
succeeded his father and became Squire. The death duties
which were levied on the death of Sir Fairfax were drastic-
ally heavy and therefore economies had to be introduced
both on the Estate and in the gardens. At this time, Mr.
Brown, the head gardener, having attained the age of
seventy years, decided to retire, whereupon Mr. Cartwright
invited me to take his place, and operate with a reduced
staff, and for the first time we were required to sell all
surplus produce to supplement the upkeep of the gardens.

During my initial years as head gardener I was not expected to make a profit from the produce I grew. The main
aim was to keep expenditure down. However, the larger my
profits the more funds were available for the upkeep of the
greenhouses. With this in mind I quickly cultivated a local
market for the surplus produce, fruit, flowers and vegetables.

No peaches or nectarines were sold locally however, as they were dispatched to Covent Garden Market.

The most important factor in those days was that of time. It would have been pointless to have grown hundreds of plants, when I had neither the time nor labour to look after them properly. Also as I intended to sell direct to the public my produce required to be superior to that sold in the shops, and therefore quality was of paramount importance.

Home-grown tomatoes were in great demand and so I decided to grow them in the old vine and peach borders. A start was made in January when the seed was sown one inch apart in boxes. The seedlings when ready were transplanted into large 60 size pots and later into six-inch pots ready for planting in the borders in April. These provided my early crop. A second sowing made during February provided good sturdy plants for the borders. A third and fourth sowing during March provided plants for sale. I always took care not to crowd the plants and left plenty of space between them so that I could move quickly and easily between the rows. To ensure that the borders would be clear in time to transplant chrysanthemums I stopped the first sown tomatoes after the fifth truss of bloom, and the second batch after the fourth truss. I always took care to prepare my compost in advance and I waited until it had warmed through before using it for potting the young plants. This preparation is essential as failure to warm the compost to approximately the same temperature as that in which the young plants will be growing causes a severe check on the plants.

Often whilst working outside one would be driven inside by a sudden storm and whenever such an occasion arose, I took the opportunity whilst preparing my compost to heat some bricks in the boiler fire before placing them amongst the compost. In no time at all the compost was nicely warmed through and ready for use. The chrysanthemums which were left in the tomato borders during the winter supplied an abundance of strong rooted cuttings which were then planted singly in large 60 size pots before being planted in an outside border specially prepared for them. A space of two feet was allowed between each plant, and the rows were three feet apart. A square shaped excavation was prepared for each plant with the spade and was filled in with prepared compost. The chrysanthemums were planted about three inches below ground level, thus enabling me to water in sufficient quantities when necessary. Several times during the season I took the spade and cut around each plant in the same place as the original excavation. By so doing I ensured that when lifting time arrived the plant would come away with a good mass of soil adhering to it. The Christmas and later varieties of chrysanthemums were potted into ten-inch pots, so that if it became necessary they could be transferred to the warm house.

Early potatoes were another good paying crop and provided I could start lifting at least a fortnight before the villagers I could sell as many as I could grow. I commenced planting in March, and as soon as the potatoes showed above the ground level I covered them each night with a thin layer of straw. One year I saved my crop after a frost by spraying them with cold water a little in advance of the sun. Another year we experienced very sharp frost towards the end of May. The potatoes were about a foot high and on examining the garden on the following day it was very distressing to see the damage sustained by the various crops. The potatoes were cut down level with the ground, and as I did not have the time or labour to replant them they were allowed to remain in the ground. Two to three weeks later a mass of young growths appeared so that they almost covered the ground. Having nothing to lose I decided to thin them in the same way as I would any seedling that had become overcrowded and leave three or four of the strongest growths on each plant. When lifting time arrived the results were really amazing. I harvested one of the best crops of early potatoes I had seen for years, and as new potatoes were naturally scarce that year I made a handsome profit from my surprise crop.

Just prior to the death of Sir Fairfax Cartwright a new

roof was erected over the peach houses. This meant that I acquired the old lights, each of which measured eight feet by three feet nine inches. These I used to force young carrots and lettuce in the raised outside vine border which was ideal for this purpose. Besides carrots and lettuce I also grew radishes and the small silver skinned onion for an early crop. In addition I sowed brussels sprouts, cabbage and cauliflower, for transplanting. These always brought in a quick return, as did the lettuce thinnings. As soon as the plants had grown large enough, I dispensed with the lights which I used to make another makeshift frame for bedding and other plants. A frame situated on a sunny sheltered border is of great value to any gardener, and the simplest materials are suitable for this purpose. For instance a few boards, a length of 500 gauge polythene and a box of drawing pins are sufficient for the quick erection of such a frame, which can be invaluable when space is taken up in the greenhouse for tomatoes, or it is being used for the hardening off of bedding plants.

Apart from some casual labour during the evenings and week-ends my permanent labour force consisted of one man in the pleasure grounds, one man in the kitchen garden, and a high spirited boy who was fond of practical jokes. My kitchen garden man was affectionately known as Old George. He was a great help and had worked in the gardens long before I started work there. His father had also worked in the kitchen garden for about 60 years, and therefore I was able to gain first hand knowledge of what had happened not only in the gardens, but also in the village, for almost the last hundred years.

It had always been an unwritten law in the gardens that no fruit or vegetables were allowed to waste or be thrown away and whenever there was a surplus the men were permitted to take it home. Conditions were now different, as the surplus produce was being sold for the first time. Whilst I would naturally frown on anything being taken without permission I did not enforce the new conditions very vigorously, as I had always been aware that Old George occasionally took small items to his two sisters, one of whom was an invalid. This practice had become accepted over the years. The boy was also aware of George's little secret and he used to watch carefully for an opportunity to play one of his frequent practical jokes. George was often the butt of his fiendish pranks and some of these remain

vividly imprinted in my mind. On one occasion whilst gathering peas George placed some pods carefully in his lunch handkerchief, afterwards hiding them in an outhouse until it was time for him to go home. Unfortunately for him and his sisters the boy had found them and shelled each one before returning the empty pods to the hiding place. On another occasion George hid some apples in a hole in the wall of the outer shed and inevitably the boy discovered them. He found that by standing on a box he could reach into this new hiding place, and so he removed the fruit and substituted a baited mouse-trap. I never knew what happened when George went to collect his apples but the next morning the mouse-trap was found on the ground smashed into little pieces. Another incident which I remember well occurred whilst a crop of potatoes was being lifted. The boy came into the greenhouse where I was working, laughing to himself, and on my enquiring what amused him so, he told me that Old George had hidden some potatoes in a heap of wood ashes. He asked me if I would like to see them, and out of curiosity I went with him to the hiding place, and the boy shifted the wood ashes to expose just over a dozen perfect potatoes, and then even I was compelled to laugh. The boy had painted the potatoes green. George must have been furious when he returned to collect his carefully selected potatoes, for a flower show was scheduled in one of the neighbouring villages in the next day or so, and there was little doubt that had it not been for the boy's unwelcome efforts, George would have taken first prize with his potatoes. I was rather sorry when the boy left, as he had decided not to make gardening his career. As he was leaving the garden on his last evening, George turned to me and said very forcibly, 'I'm going to treat myself to a few drinks to-night now that young b——— has gone.'

There was a considerable amount of digging to be carried out in the kitchen garden and I often took up the spade to help. I always found it disheartening after working hard for a few hours to glance behind and see the large expanse still to be dug. This experience has I am sure been shared by the majority of my readers. For years I have remedied this by dividing the plot to be dug into ten yard sections, digging each section crosswise at an angle of 45 degrees. The soil excavated from the beginning of the plot is wheeled away to the opposite corner. By digging across a section I arrive at the opposite corner with only a small trench remaining about one yard long. I then commence the next section, digging away from the first section in the opposite direction, the first few spits filling the small trench left in the first section. This system I repeat until the whole plot is completed and I arrive eventually at the point where the original barrow loads of soil were tipped. I have found this idea so successful that ever since that time nearly forty years ago I have dug my borders in this way regardless of the size of the plot, always starting at the lowest corner. About this time we grubbed up an old fruit plantation and I was left with a plot of ground which was very uneven. The soil in the centre of the plot was much higher than that at the sides. To remedy this situation I started digging in a similar way starting at the lowest corner, but instead of digging crosswise I dug around in a circular fashion, finally leaving myself standing on about a square yard of soil in the centre of the plot. This method which I adopted has recently been vividly brought back to my mind when walking around some of the new building estates. In a later chapter I will write how I overcame some of the difficulties in clearing and levelling such sites.

CHAPTER THIRTEEN

My Peaches

THE PEACH IS GENERALLY SUPPOSED TO HAVE originated in China, where it was recorded over two thousand years before its introduction to the Romans. We grew four varieties of peaches and four varieties of nectarines at Aynhoe, all fan trained. One of the glories of growing peaches is their bloom, the mass of pink blossom well worth going to see if you get the chance. First I will deal with the nectarine, which is after all a variety of peach. There are in fact recorded instances of a nectarine originating from the seed of a peach and vice versa. Visually the main difference between the two fruits is that the nectarine has a smooth tough skin, usually green and red, whilst the peach has a furry softer skin, usually pink and yellow. The varieties of nectarine which we grew were:–

Elruge, a medium sized fruit of excellent flavour. This is a very old variety and was known before 1670. Its name is said to be an anagram of that of its raiser, a nurseryman of Hoxlon in the reign of Charles II. Pineapple, a large fruit having a delicious flavour, and, as its name implies, not unlike that of a pineapple, is one of the best nectarines, and was raised by a Mr. Rivers. Humbolt, also raised by Mr. Rivers, was a large fruit, tender and juicy. Lord Napier, a juicy, rich flavoured fruit, was raised from the seed of an Early Albert Peach and introduced in 1869.

The peaches we grew were:–

Duke of York, a large, crimson coloured fruit, very refreshing with a tender flesh, and raised by Mr. Rivers. Peregrine, also raised by Mr. Rivers, and first introduced in 1906, is certainly one of the best and handsomest of peaches with flesh very mellow and juicy. Waterloo, an excellent variety for early forcing, was raised by Mr. Lish at Waterloo, U.S.A., and introduced into this country by Mr. Rivers. Nectarine peach, a fine autumn variety for the cool greenhouse, is a large fruit, tender and juicy and of good flavour when well grown.

It is popularly believed that of the two, the nectarine has the better flavour. In my opinion this belief arises from the fact that the nectarine, even when it is picked under-ripe, retains its flavour over a much longer period. The peach is only first class for two or three days and therefore considerable experience is necessary to assess when it is at its best. When it is I believe that there is no fruit to equal it.

When they are to be sold, peaches are picked whilst they are still firm and under-ripe. They ripen afterwards during marketing, but the flavour is not always good. For home consumption the fruit should be left on the tree as long as possible, and should be inspected regularly, as often as three times a day if possible. When examining the fruit, the palm of the hand should be placed carefully beneath the peach whilst the fruit is tested for firmness with a finger of the other hand at a point where the fruit joins the branch. If it is possible to make a slight depression without undue pressure, then the peach is ready to be picked, and this is done by an upward movement and a sharp twist. In this way the fruit will come away without bruising. Fruit should never be allowed to fall from the tree, because apart from severe bruising, it will have passed its best and lost its flavour.

One day whilst browsing through a gardening journal, I read of a peach, Sea Eagle, at Ketton Hall, which had produced a fruit weighing sixteen ounces. Also at the same nurseries a peach, Nectarine, had been grown which weighed fourteen ounces and measured twelve inches in circumference. As I also grew this latter variety I decided to see if I could improve on this specimen, and in 1938 I succeeded in producing a Nectarine peach which weighed fourteen and three-quarter ounces. I sent the fruit to the offices of the *Gardener's Chronicle*, accompanied by a report which was later published, and in which I stated that I would be interested to learn of larger or heavier fruit of this variety. In fact I received no reply to this challenge.

In July of that year I exhibited a box of Nectarine peaches and a box of Pineapple nectarines before the Fruit & Vegetable Committee of the Royal Horticultural Society in London, and I was awarded a Certificate of Cultural Commendation. The fruit was reported to be of superb quality. One of the judges sitting on the Committee was the late Mr. C. H. Middleton who was well known for his gardening broadcasts on radio. Soon afterwards I was honoured when he visited me at Aynhoe.

Many readers will I am sure recall Mr. Middleton's ready wit which highlighted his broadcasts and made them so interesting. During his visit to Aynhoe I was to learn that he had inherited this gift from his father.

Mr. Middleton had spent all of two hours with me in the garden during which time we had become deeply engrossed in our common interests, when suddenly he exclaimed 'I don't know what my father will say, I left him in the car telling him I would only be away for a short while.' We returned to the car and Mr. Middleton introduced me to his father, at the same time apologising for his long absence. Smiling, his father said 'Not at all my boy, I've just been for a stroll around the village.' Mr. Middleton senior who was well over eighty years of age was unable to leave the car unaided. It was through Mr. Middleton that I was later introduced to Mr. Freddie Grisewood of T.V. and radio fame, who counted gardening amongst his many interests.

In August 1939 at the Royal Horticultural Society Hall, I staged an exhibit consisting of twelve dishes of Peregrine peaches and nine dishes of Pineapple nectarines. For this exhibit I was awarded the Silver Hogg Memorial medal for what was described as *An exhibit of magnificent Peaches and Nectarines, all of which were of first rate exhibition appearance, and set out very attractively.*

The importance of presenting exhibits attractively at any show cannot be stressed too strongly, and for the benefit of readers who show their produce, I will reconstruct this particular exhibit.

I covered the space allotted to me with moss on three different levels. On these stagings I placed the twenty-one identical plates, and on each plate I had placed a layer of cotton wool covered with good healthy peach leaves. Each plate contained eight or nine fruit, the average weight of the peaches being ten ounces, and the nectarines eight ounces. In between each plate I placed a small pot of *asparagus plumosus* fern, and around the entire staging at six-inch intervals I arranged small pots of the hanging fern *asparagus Sprengeri*, all the pots being immersed in moss.

At the conclusion of the show I packed the fruit which was still firm ready for sale the following morning at Covent Garden Market. A few of the fruit had become over-ripe, and as far as I was concerned were quite useless. As I discarded one over-ripe fruit beneath the staging, I heard a voice beside me deploring my wastefulness. On looking up I saw a policeman standing near. He informed me that as soon as he had cleared the public from the Hall, he was off duty, and he would dearly have liked to have taken one of the peaches which I was discarding home to his wife. I duly presented the law with two peaches but explained to him that I had nothing in which to pack them. This problem was soon resolved however, when the officer calmly removed his helmet, placed the two ripe fruit carefully on his head, gingerly replaced his helmet, and then turned and

walked very slowly and stiffly from the Hall. I have often wondered whether the peaches reached their destination safely.

A few days after the show I received a congratulatory letter from Mr. Wood, director of the well known Taplow seedsmen of that name. He wrote saying that he had missed the show and had therefore not had the pleasure of seeing my exhibit. However, he continued, *the Silver Hogg medal tells its own tale. These are not given away very readily by the Council. What a pity you could not tell a little story of how it was done.* Perhaps this is a good opportunity to do just that.

Firstly, no effort was spared in procuring a well drained root run for the trees, and in providing suitable soil. Whenever a new tree was required we would remove all the existing soil to a depth of three feet or more until we reached the concrete base which sloped towards a main drain. This allowed all surplus water to drain freely away, and also prevented the roots from pushing down into the cold uncongenial sub-soil.

The concrete base was then covered with drainage material, consisting of broken bricks, to a depth of nine inches, and on top of this material was placed freshly cut fibrous turves, with the grass facing downwards. A compost was then added, and this was well trodden down making a layer of about one foot in depth. The compost used consisted of three parts chopped turf, which had been stacked previously for about six months, and one part old mortar rubble. To this was added a medium sized potful of half-inch bones, the whole being thoroughly mixed together. When this was completed the bed was well watered and then left for several days.

It is perhaps worth mentioning here the method we used when stacking turves for future use in composts. Between each layer of turves which were cut from the park land on the Estate were inserted alternate layers of well rotted manure and old soot (at least twelve months old). This operation continued until we had built a sizeable stack, sufficient for our needs during the next twelve months.

After the bed had been thoroughly soaked and left for several days to settle, a large flat stone was placed on the spot where the tree was to be planted. This was done to prevent the main roots from going straight down, and the benefit of this operation is derived should root pruning or replanting become necessary at a later date. The compost which was finally used consisted of three parts chopped loam and one part old mortar rubble to which was added a liberal amount of wood ash or charcoal, and a medium sized potful of coarse bonemeal. The whole mixture was put through a one-inch sieve before it was used, and again the compost was well trodden down and watered, after which at least two weeks were allowed to elapse in order that the compost might settle and warm up. At the end of this period the tree was finally planted. This operation must be carried out carefully, the area excavated to receive the tree being a little larger than the actual roots of the tree.

From this point onwards the aim must be to produce a well-balanced and fruitful tree, and to achieve this, correct pruning is essential. The peach bears fruit only on one-year shoots, and it is therefore necessary each year to ensure that the tree has plenty of these shoots. Quite early in the season, buds begin to break along the whole length of the shoot. These are known as growth buds and fruit buds. Two things have to be considered at this time, firstly the production of fruit, and secondly the provision of young growth needed to carry the following year's harvest, because after bearing fruit a growth never fruits again, and unless it is needed to extend the tree or to take the place of a much older shoot it is useless and should be cut out immediately.

When the shoots begin to break into growth and reach a length of approximately half an inch, a number of them must be removed to prevent the tree from becoming overcrowded. This should be done carefully and thoughtfully however, and too many growths should not be removed at one time, as this would probably upset the balance of sap to the tree. This operation should finally result in well placed growths on either side of the tree, and one growth at the top of the shoot to draw up the sap and extend the tree. When the extension of the tree ceases to become necessary, the top growth should be stopped after the fourth leaf.

The blossom when under glass needs to be artificially pollinated, and the most effective way of carrying out this operation is to use a rabbit's tail affixed to the end of a cane. Pollination should continue until the fruit is set, and during this time on very sunny days a light syringing of the trees with rain water is beneficial.

Thinning out of the fruit must commence as soon as the flowers have set, and at this stage a decision must be made as to the amount of fruit the tree can reasonably carry. I usually allow one fruit to each square foot of space. The first thinning should leave four to five fruit on each shoot, and the final thinning out process should take place after the stoning period. It is always as well to remember that it is preferable to have one super fruit than three or four small ones.

During the stoning period the trees should not be forced in any way. The method I use to determine the end of this

stoning period is to take an unwanted fruit and cut it in
half with a sharp knife, and when I find that this operation
becomes difficult I know that this particular phase is almost
over. The borders are then dressed with well decayed cow
manure to a depth of about three inches, and this is well
watered in, and then throughout the growing season the
trees are syringed both morning and evening, making
certain that both sides of the leaves are similarly treated. The
syringing continues right up until the time when the fruit
begins to ripen. During very hot dry spells of weather, the
borders and paths were soaked down several times each day,
and this treatment continued even after the syringing had
ceased.

After the fruit has been harvested, the syringing treatment is recommenced and is continued until the fall of the
leaf. This use of the syringe not only keeps the trees healthy
but it also keeps the red spider at bay.

During the autumn the borders were again soaked, as this
is the time when the fruit buds for the following year
begin to swell, and failure to supply sufficient water to the
roots at this time will inevitably lead to serious bud dropping
in the spring. It is worth remembering that borders under
glass receive only what they are given, and furthermore
evaporation is far greater inside than outside.

When the leaves have fallen, any pruning which was not
carried out when the fruit was picked should then be undertaken, making certain that all the resulting cuts are painted
with styptic. By planning carefully and retaining plenty of
young shoots at the base of the tree, it may be possible if
overcrowding is imminent to dispense with a large branch.

When the pruning had been completed, all the remaining
branches were cut loose from their guide wires, and washed
down with an insecticide. The branches were then secured
together whilst the house was thoroughly washed and hosed
down. The walls were lime washed, after which the branches
were loosely tied back in position.

In December the borders were lightly pricked over with a
hand fork, and all loose soil was raked off. A top dressing

of prepared compost was then applied, similar to that in which the trees were originally planted, after which no further attention was necessary until the spring when the buds began to burst, and the cycle was put into operation once more.

I referred earlier to the process of root pruning. This becomes necessary only when a tree becomes rank thereby resulting in loss of fruit. Should this happen, the method used is to excavate a two-foot trench about four feet from the trunk of the tree, continuing the trench half way around the tree. When this has been done, carefully work under the tree cutting off all the roots which are growing downwards. Carry on with this process until the flat stone upon which the tree is resting is located, and then replace the soil which has been removed with freshly prepared compost, and make firm. Should the tree continue to make rank growth the following year, the same operation should be carried out to the other half of the tree.

In one of the large peach houses at Aynhoe, figs were also grown. We always found it necessary before planting a fig to brick off the surrounding area thus preventing the roots from spreading into the adjacent borders. Unlike the peach the fig did not require manuring, but it did need a far greater volume of water.

CHAPTER FOURTEEN

Before the Glory Faded

ALTHOUGH DURING THE 1920'S AND EARLY' 30'S I was concentrating more and more on bedding plants and growing tomatoes, in my spare time I began to develop an interest in hybridising and raising new plants, and I began to extend my knowledge on orchid growing.

The new Squire still retained his rooms in the smaller Grammar House where he lived for the next few years with his mother. During this time, he formed a cricket team, chiefly from the village and the Estate, to compete with teams from neighbouring counties. One fixture which always created great enthusiasm was the annual contest with the Northants County Police. The part of the Park where the cricket matches took place was known as Ryland Hill. The Lime Avenue passed through this field and provided a very picturesque setting for the cricket. This field was regularly plagued by moles, and to prevent these creatures from ruining the playing area with their burrowing, it became necessary to lay a large expanse of half-inch wire netting beneath the turf forming the pitch.

Mr. Cartwright, who was president of the Fire Brigade, arranged an annual party, to be held on New Year's Eve. No expense was spared on these memorable and lavish occasions, and they were eagerly anticipated by all those fortunate enough to receive an invitation. Each member of the brigade was allowed to invite a lady companion. In addition, the president invited many others, my wife and I being amongst the fortunate ones. On the day preceding the party, together with some Estate men, we would transform the Fire Station with flowers and evergreens into a Festive Hall. The popularity of this event increased year by year, and with members of other brigades being invited, it became necessary to hold the party in the newly built Village Hall, only a few yards from the Fire Station.

This party takes my mind back to my early years in the gardens, helping to run out the hoses for fire drill on alternate Friday mornings. All the men on the Estate were required to attend. At that time, the fire engine consisted of the old wooden manual type. A complement of eight men were needed to man the pump, four men on either side, and during practice drills, this antique but nevertheless effective apparatus projected a powerful stream of water well above the Park House roof. Ironically, this faithful old relic of the past was itself destroyed by fire in 1933, when a large fire broke out in the timber yard and spread rapidly to adjacent buildings.

A few years previously, Mr. Cartwright had bought a new trailer type of fire engine, a Merryweather, to supplement the old hand-operated machine, and he formed an official Fire Brigade, recruiting men from the Estate and village. Although the Brigade was a private one, it was affiliated to the County Fire Brigade Association. The men received a five shilling turning out fee, and five shillings an hour for time spent in dealing with the fire. For many years, the members accepted only the turning out fee, and the re-remainder was deposited in the bank to form a fund to provide for the next of kin on the death of a member. The amount by which a dependant benefited was fifty pounds and this is still paid up to the present time, although the Brigade has long ceased to exist. At the time of this book going to print, there are only six surviving members, my brother and my cousin amongst them.

Soon after the outbreak of the Second World War, the Aynhoe Brigade, in common with other private brigades throughout the country, was disbanded, and all fire fighting duties were taken over by the National Fire Service, and were controlled by the respective County or County Borough Councils. The Aynhoe engine was commandeered and taken over by a unit at Deddington, a large neighbouring village, and so a long tradition came to an end.

In 1932 the Squire began to entertain again in the Park House, and later that year he married Elspeth, only daughter of Lord and Lady Weir.

The newly married couple moved into the Park House together with their servants, and we were back in business again. Extra plants were required, particularly large specimen plants. Two large glass houses were re-connected to the hot water system, and once again I had the task of building up a collection of plants suitable for decorating a large house.

Additional bedding plants were needed to fill many new flower beds which were made in the pleasure grounds. One of these new beds was made on the roof of the Ice House which was stripped of its turf, four terraced walls being constructed around it surmounted by one round bed on the topmost part. In autumn these terraces were planted with wallflowers and myosotis, with aubrieta and double arabis draping the fifteen-inch high walls, whilst in the summer months plants left over from the formal beds were planted there, such as geraniums, heliotrope, stocks, asters, antirrhinums, petunias, dwarf dahlias, marigolds, nemesia and lobelia. Thus this bed always provided a mass of colour which was particularly striking to the stranger walking from the Park House towards the Lime Avenue walk.

We grew about two thousand antirrhinums for bedding

purposes. The seed was sown in January, and when the small seedlings were ready they were transplanted, about twenty at a time into six-inch pots. After the third pair of leaves had formed on each plant, the tops were pinched out so that eventually sturdy bushy plants were produced. They were then stood in a cold frame. At the end of March we sowed the petunia seed; a very thin sowing of this seed is sufficient. By the time these seedlings were ready for transplanting, the antirrhinums had been removed from their pots and in turn transplanted to a sheltered border facing south, where they remained until they were required for bedding out. The pots were then washed and re-crocked and used straight away to transplant the petunias, eight seedlings being allocated to each six-inch pot.

I discovered that by using deep pots instead of the usual shallow boxes, the plants experienced less check when the planting out time arrived. Geraniums, heliotrope and dwarf dahlias were grown singly in pots. Asters, lobelia, marigolds, nemesia and alyssum were transplanted from seed pans into boxes and were placed one inch apart. Afterwards they were again transplanted into cold frames. A plentiful supply of beech leaf soil was always readily available, and therefore beds were made up of this compost in the cold frames ready to receive the seedlings, which meant that we were able to allocate more space for each seedling than we could otherwise have done if we had had to rely solely on seed boxes. The extra time taken up in this operation was fully justified when bedding out time came around as the plants then needed far less watering, and furthermore they were always strong bushy specimens which when lifted retained plenty of soil on their roots.

In August 1935 I was summoned by my employers to discuss the floral arrangements which were required for an 18th-century Ball which was to be held in the Park House during November of that year. This was to be a very grand and auspicious occasion and during the ensuing weeks the production of plants for the Ball was given top priority. The normal floral decorations at the house were only continued provided they did not interfere with the plans for the Ball.

I decided that I should require approximately two hundred plants, some of which would have to be retarded and others forced to ensure that they would be at their peak when the big day arrived. Chrysanthemums in particular required special treatment, and were sprayed frequently, some with a weak solution of soot water, and others with soft water to which Epsom Salts were added at a ratio of one teaspoonful to each gallon. The chrysanthemums were by this time already in their final pots. However, many of them now had to be re-potted, and were given continual top dressings. I found during this time that by inserting a band of tin inside the top of the pot so that it overlapped and increased the the height of the container, I was able to top dress right up to the height of the pot, and at the same time water the plants sufficiently.

One variety, Louisa Pockett, fared extremely well, and as a result of twice being stopped the blooms turned to a delicate shade of pink. Two plants of this variety stood six feet tall, and each carried around fifty fine blooms, six inches in diameter. Another good variety which provided some fine large specimens was Mrs. R. Luxford. Tall single chrysanthemums also played an important part in the plan, particularly where height was important. Other plants used included orchids, one of which was *Cattleya portia* of course, Lorraine begonias, cyclamen, zonal pelargoniums, stocks and various varieties of ferns and foliage plants.

The Ball itself will long be remembered by all who took part, and by those who contributed to its organisation, and everything appertaining to the Ball was required to be strictly in keeping with the period which it represented. The courtyard was illuminated by old candle-lit lanterns, and no sooner had the different parties of guests arrived than their horseless carriages, automobiles if you prefer, were driven swiftly out of sight, as if their very presence offended and outraged all who were compelled to set their eyes upon them. No electric lighting was permitted in the house except where it was screened by banks of flowers.

Groups of plants were arranged inside all the windows overlooking the terrace at the front of the house, and before the Ball got under way these windows were shuttered with the exception of one window in each of the main rooms, which remained unshuttered to enable the villagers to walk along the terrace and witness the lavish spectacle which was taking place within. Leaving the windows unshuttered for the villagers to witness the scene inside the house was typical of that age. In Europe it might have invited thrown bricks, but here the village appreciated the gesture. Looking back I have the impression of a great house sailing like a ship with her lights blazing before the blacked out utility voyage of the great war ahead.

The food and wine provided was 18th-century down to the last detail, and the guests in their period costumes and wigs provided a glorious and colourful spectacle as they performed their minuets. A number of men employed on the Estate were enlisted as flunkeys, and looked resplendent in their green livery, although sad to relate, at the conclusion of the proceedings some of them located a few bottles of liquor which had been surplus to the guests' requirements, and which was undoubtedly more potent than the local ale, and consequently one or two very bedraggled flunkeys were found during the early hours, with wigs askew, in the most unlikely places.

When the rooms were being prepared for the Ball, the double doors between the main rooms were taken off their hinges and numbered before being stored in the cellars. All these doors were so aligned that by peering through the key-hole of the first door, you could see through all the key-holes to the far end of the house. Fortunately my brother who was one of the flunkeys in charge of the gentlemen's cloakrooms kept a clear head during the festivities, because as soon as the last guest had departed he was given the task of rehanging all doors, so that the rooms could be securely locked up for the remainder of the night.

In the years to follow, a number of large dinner parties

were held in the Park House, and the task of arranging floral displays in the house and for the dinner table became a regular one, and indeed a pleasurable one, for I grew to enjoy this part of the operation almost as much as I did growing the plants.

The centrepiece of the dining table at the Park House was a magnificent gold urn which had been presented to General Cartwright by George III. Around the urn were four Augsberg gilt salts, and four gilt candlesticks. A typical flower arrangement would be pink carnations and violets in small vases between the candlesticks, with the evergreen selaginella, a moss-like fern, tracing the table, and at intervals of three or four inches a small head of schyzanthus or violet. When illuminated at night the effect was really beautiful.

On very special occasions an extensive Meissen dinner service was taken from its large leather-lined travelling box, and laid on the table. The plates and dishes were individually and beautifully painted with views of Dresden. I understood from the butler that this priceless set had been a gift to Napoleon from the Emperor of Austria, and that it had been found by General Cartwright after it had been left behind at the battle of Waterloo.

One such occasion, when the Meissen was put on show, and when I was required to arrange a floral display in the house at very short notice, was during a short visit from the late Queen Mary. I particularly remember this event because it was early in May and the large flower beds at the entrance to the house had begun to look rather untidy. Therefore we hastily cleared away the wallflowers and mysotis, and planted in their place five hundred scarlet geraniums each in their pots, and as soon as Her Majesty had left Aynhoe, the geraniums were immediately lifted and returned to the greenhouses to await the correct bedding-out season which was three weeks later.

The plant arrangement in the house comprised cinerarias, hippeastrums, stocks, schyzanthus and a few orchids which included cattleyas. It was only necessary to purchase three dozen pink carnations and a large bunch of *Lilium longiflorum* to help decorate the dinner table, the remainder of the flowers and plants being provided by the gardens.

The Coronation in May 1937 of King George was a memorable day for Aynhoe. The whole village was decorated with flags and bunting. On both sides of the road from the Park House to the Grammar House and also around the green in front of the Cartwright Arms Hotel stood a line of barrels, painted red, white and blue. A twenty-foot pole surmounted with a large gilt crown was erected in each barrel. Flags and bunting were suspended between the poles, and three feet from the top of each pole stretched an electric cable with multi-coloured bulbs every few feet. On the wall of a house in the village square was displayed a large painted Union Jack illuminated with electric bulbs. At night visitors flocked into the village from many miles around to admire the illuminations.

The Squire provided a high tea for the inhabitants in the Village Hall and following the banquet each tenant was presented with an inscribed album containing photographs of the village decorations as a memento of a very special day in the village. I often glance through my own album and am reminded of the carnival mood which existed at Aynhoe in those last days of peace-time Britain.

CHAPTER FIFTEEN

Showing at the Hall

WHENEVER PEOPLE REFER TO THE HOUSE they usually mean The Houses of Parliament. To gardeners The Hall means The Royal Horticultural Society's Hall in Vincent Square, London.

It was in January 1938 that I first entered an exhibit at the Royal Horticultural Society Hall in London. At that time I possessed an orchid plant which boasted more than the usual quota of blooms. A gardening friend suggested that I should show the plant in London, and informed me that I could forward it direct to the Secretary of the Society by rail, and as he would be attending the show he undertook to arrange for the plant's safe return. I was rather dubious but nevertheless I agreed, and I was very pleasantly surprised when my friend returned from the show and informed me that I had been successful at my very first attempt, and had been awarded a Certificate of Cultural Commendation for what was described as a specially well grown specimen of *Laelia anceps*.

The Certificate of Cultural Commendation is awarded to a grower whose plant shows evidence of special cultural skill, whereas an Award of Merit is awarded to a plant which is a distinct advance on its predecessors. The Certificate of Cultural Commendation is thought by many to be secondary to the Award of Merit. For the commercial grower this may be so. However, I have been successful in attaining both awards on a number of occasions, and as a gardener I rank them equal in importance. The likelihood of the average gardener producing an Award of Merit plant is very rare, but the honour of securing a Certificate of Cultural Commendation is open to all. Another interesting point is that Awards of Merit and medals are always delivered to the plant's owner, whereas Certificates of Cultural Commendation are awarded to and sent direct to the gardener. I have been fortunate in this respect in having an employer who has always allowed me to retain all awards.

My success with *Laelia anceps* encouraged me to try again, this time with a hippeastrum, or as it was more commonly known, amaryllis.

I have always been an ardent admirer of hippeastrums, and therefore when I became head gardener, I bought one plant with pink flowers and a few seedlings for the sum of £5, and then together with two plants which I already possessed I began to raise my own seedlings. Immediately the seed pods burst, and the actual seeds are visible, the sooner they are sown the better. I placed twelve seeds upright in a four-inch pot, using a compost of sterilised leaf soil, peat, silver sand, and a small quantity of crushed charcoal. I prefer to sow in pots rather than pans or boxes because it simplifies the operation of turning out the seedlings, and separating them without damaging the roots.

The seedlings when ready are re-potted singly into small pots, using a compost of sterilised fibrous loam, leaf soil, peat, decayed cow manure, silver sand and a little crushed charcoal, the whole mixture being rubbed through a half-inch sieve. Each pot is then plunged into a bed of peat in a temperature ranging from 60 to 70 degrees Fahrenheit. It is the natural wish of the gardener to see his seedlings flower in the shortest possible time, and therefore the application of bottom heat is an advantage, as the plant should continue to grow without check, and must never be allowed to become root-bound until it is in its final flowering size pot.

As soon as the roots reach the side of the container it is time to re-pot, taking care to disturb the roots as little as possible. Sometimes a top dressing will suffice and can take the place of re-potting.

When the seedlings increase in size more loam can be added to the compost, which I made up of three parts fibrous loam, one part leaf soil and one part decayed cow manure, to which I added a small amount of mortar rubble, a similar amount of silver sand and crushed charcoal, and a slightly smaller amount of bonemeal.

I have found through experience that it is the small details which make all the difference between producing a fine healthy plant and a sickly one. I consider that the two most important factors in the cultivation of any plant are watering and keeping the plant clean. Cleanliness cannot be stressed too strongly. If a plant is not clean it is not healthy.

I ensured that my hippeastrums were clean by syringing them on all possible occasions, and each month I sprayed them with insecticide after first removing the dead scales from the bulbs, and using a small brush to clean the crevices. As I was unable to devote a separate house to the hippeastrums, I also took the precaution of fumigating the green-house which they occupied once a month. It is surprising what little time is taken up completing these tasks provided they are done in a systematic manner.

Eventually the pots will become full of roots and when this happens the plants can be fed with liquid manure and be given an occasional top dressing. January is usually the best time for this; the plants should be thoroughly soaked and the top soil removed and replaced with a good rich dressing. When the plants are fully grown they can be re-potted approximately every four years.

When the flowers begin to fade, they should be broken off, leaving the main stem to wither naturally. This undoubtedly assists in building up the bulbs for the following year's flower spike.

As the flowering time approaches the plants can be fed liberally for about two months, for instance Clay's fertiliser for one week followed by cow manure water for another week and then soot water, and so on. During this time the plants should be given all the sun possible. Towards autumn however water should be gradually withheld, thus allowing the bulbs to rest, but as with cyclamen, water should not be withheld completely.

Many of the hippeastrum bulbs at Aynhoe threw two spikes of bloom, and the majority of spikes carried four blooms, most of which measured about eight to ten inches in diameter, therefore these plants, which also have fine leaves, were most useful for house decoration, and were much admired, whatever time of the year they chose to flower. The bulbs themselves were very large, for instance, Snow White, which was a great success when shown at the R.H.S. Hall, had a bulb measuring fifteen inches in circumference. Some of my seedlings have flowered less than eighteen months from the date of sowing. However this is an exception to the rule for they usually require two to three years. If attention is paid to the small details amateurs will find that the hippeastrum is one of the easiest of plants to hybridise and grow. Unfortunately its popularity declined in the immediate post war years, but I am very pleased to note that they are now becoming popular again.

The special attention and care I took over raising my hippeastrums was handsomely rewarded when I exhibited my best plants at the R.H.S. Hall at Westminster. I exhibited my first hippeastrum on 22nd February 1938. I had named it Edward Cartwright after my employer's only son. It was awarded an Award of Merit and was described as being a fine seedling with large bright Tyrian rose flowers of good shape with veins of a deeper colour.

On November 8th of the same year, I showed a pure white

seedling named Snow White. This title was inspired by the fact that the film *Snow White and the Seven Dwarfs* was being shown at this time. Described by the Committee as a splendid white variety in which the clear whiteness is relieved by a touch of green at the base of the segments, it also gained an Award of Merit.

Five months later I exhibited yet another seedling, this time named after myself. Awarding the plant an Award of Merit, the Committee reported *E. Humphris is an excellent white variety of good form with a touch of green at the base of the segments*. A gardening journal reported it as being *a strong white variety of great purity, which for substance and shape left nothing to be desired*.

My collection of hippeastrums includes the variety Susan which I understand received an Award of Merit in 1936. In fact from that time until the latter part of 1940 when hostilities forced the R.H.S. Hall to close for the duration, my seedlings were the only hippeastrums to receive Award of Merit Certificates.

In April of 1940 I exhibited a group of hippeastrums in the R.H.S. Hall, for which I was awarded the Silver Banksian Medal.

In the long history of our gardens few men have been able to exert such a wide and beneficial influence in their development as was wielded by Sir Joseph Banks throughout the long reign of George III. Sir Joseph who was born in 1743 and died in 1820 was always on friendly terms with the Royal Family, so also were The Hon. Charles Greville and General Cartwright. I feel sure under those circumstances that these men all interested in horticulture must have met. I prize the Banksian Medal very highly partly because of this link with the distant past. At about this time I received an interesting letter from a Mr. J. D. Mitchell of Sebring, Florida, U.S.A., who having read of my collection, and wishing to improve his own stock, enquired whether I could spare some of my Award of Merit varieties.

Unfortunately I had been forced to destroy all my surplus stock owing to the war, which had forced me to concentrate

mainly on food production, and had deprived me of most
of my labour force, and I was therefore obliged to reply to
Mr. Mitchell informing him with regret that I was unable to
provide the specimens he required. He answered my letter
saying that he fully understood my difficulties, and concluded *Yours for Victory, J. D. Mitchell.*

During the latter part of 1938 I embarked upon a correspondence course with the International Correspondence
School with a view to gaining the National Diploma in
Horticulture. Unfortunately I never sat for my examination
because in 1940, having to tend to the gardens virtually on my
own, I was unable to find the time to continue my studies.
Also I had enlisted in the Home Guard, in which I was
eventually commissioned, being placed in charge of the
Company's Picket Mortar team. I derived great satisfaction
from this new pastime, but it took up a great deal of what
little spare time I had. During the time that I did study, I
completed 23 test papers, for which the lowest percentage
mark I received was 80%. For the majority of the papers I
was awarded over 90% and for a paper on Botany Plant
Form & Function I gained 100 marks. I often regret that I
was unable to have completed my course, and eventually
have taken an examination, but nevertheless the research I
carried out to assist me in my studies has often proved
valuable since.

In April 1939, I was contemplating whether or not to
show three specimen plants of calceolaria. The largest of
these plants, which was growing in a ten-inch pot, carried
approximately six hundred blooms most of which averaged
three inches in diameter. These plants together formed a
splendid mass of colour. At this time I received a visit from
a friend of mine who was also a Fellow of the Royal Horticultural Society. On learning that I was considering exhibiting
the plants, he expressed the opinion that he doubted
whether the Floral Committee would grant an award to the
plants bearing in mind that they were comparatively young
plants, and he further doubted whether they would travel
without becoming too damaged. However, having nothing

to lose I decided to carry out a test, and on the Saturday prior to the show, I placed the largest of the three plants, which as it so happened had been in bloom longer than the others, in a wooden container which I then transferred to my car. I drove several miles along the surrounding country roads, intentionally choosing those thoroughfares which were poorly metalled. To make the test even more stringent I purposely drove over pot holes, and also braked sharply, so that the box containing the plant was thrown suddenly forward. Surprisingly the plant appeared to have suffered little damage, and a further inspection on Monday morning revealed that the plant had shed no blooms, although a few had become slightly damaged, but in view of the rough treatment they had received this was hardly surprising. I decided the risk of taking them to London was warranted, and so at 5 a.m. the following morning I set off in my car, and drove carefully towards London, arriving at the R.H.S. Hall at 9 a.m. The plants had arrived safely and were greatly admired by those who attended the show. Notwithstanding my friend's somewhat gloomy forecast I was awarded a Certificate of Cultural Commendation for the plants which were described as *Three magnificent specimen pot plants of Calceolaria Victoria Prize Strain.*

The compost used for the cultivation of calceolarias is similar to that used for hippeastrums. The seed is sown in early May and I always took the precaution of standing the seed pan on an inverted pot which was stood in water. This protected the seedlings from slugs and mice. Calceolarias must be grown in cool conditions at all times, and shaded from hot sunshine.

The 16th April 1940 was the last time I was able to exhibit plants at the R.H.S. Hall before it was closed for the duration of the war. On this occasion, besides the group of hippeastrums which I have already mentioned, I took with me three plants of regal pelargonium, reasoning that I might possibly gain a Certificate of Cultural Commendation if I was lucky, and in fact this was to be, but I received a very pleasant surprise when the plants were also given an Award of Merit. The R.H.S. report said of the plants, *A very hand-some Pelargonium from an unnamed seedling. The large rounded flowers with crinkled edges are borne in well-formed trusses. The upper petals are Tyrian rose-feathered and blotched with crimson maroon, the lower petals are rosy carmine.* The Certificate of Cultural Commendation was awarded for exceptionally well grown plants.

CHAPTER SIXTEEN
The Tunnel of War

O N THE IST OF JULY 1940, ON MR. CART-
wright's suggestion, I began to run the greenhouses
and kitchen garden on my own account as a market
garden, and this agreement was to continue for the duration
of the war. Naturally I began to concentrate more on the
production of food. Plants normally used for house decoration to which so much time had been devoted gave way to
tomato plants, and reluctantly other adjustments had to be
made. For the first few months I was entirely without labour
and compelled to rely on assistance from my wife and son,
who was still attending school.

My past experiences when I first became head gardener
were invaluable to me at that time, and enabled me to
implement the necessary changes without delay. The first
thing I did was to refer to some old diaries in which were
recorded details of all the work carried out in June and
July during my early days at the gardens.

Every Sunday evening I made it my practice to walk through the greenhouses and around the kitchen garden and make notes of the tasks that needed to be carried out during the ensuing week. From these notes I compiled a list of tasks which I pinned up in the potting shed, each task being crossed off when accomplished. Whenever I had some spare time, whether it was an hour or only a few minutes, I was able to consult the list and select a task which could be completed in the time I had available.

The kitchen garden was divided up by a pattern of grass paths three feet in width. When labour had not been a problem they had always been regularly mown. During my first year as a market gardener however I made the mistake of allowing the grass to grow until eventually I was obliged to cut it with a scythe. This turned out to be a gigantic task and I realised that the hours spent cutting down the grass and clearing away afterwards averaged far more than a weekly trip with the lawn mower, and consequently the following year I started on the paths early in the season using a twelve-inch lawn mower without the grass box and continued to do so throughout the season. Edging out the paths was carried out twice during the season, in the late autumn using a line and spade and in the late spring with the edging shears, for this operation cutting whilst the turf was crisp with the frost, as this method bruised the edges of the path so that they did not grow so quickly thereafter. Another task I carried out during frosty weather when the surface of the soil was hard, was to scrape off the weeds on vacant plots, a job I often carried out by moonlight. This simplified matters when it came to digging, and eliminated the inconvenience of removing and burying weeds.

With the aid of a little casual labour during the summer evenings I was able to grub up the beech and privet hedge surrounding the frame-yard and this saved valuable time taken in clipping twice each year and also released extra land for food production. Another labour saving idea I utilised when preparing my seed beds was that after roughly levelling the ground with a large rake I dug narrow trenches about fifteen inches deep at intervals around the plot, and as I continued to level the bed I raked all the stones into the trenches. This system of burying them was far quicker than collecting them up and wheeling away. This idea may be helpful to some of my readers who have stony ground or even builders' rubbish to contend with. Bury the lot.

During the summer months I took the opportunity of collecting several barrow loads of fine dusty soil which I stored in a dry shed. Mixed with dry wood ashes or a little lime the soil was used when required as a thin layer on the seeds beds prior to drawing out the drills. This enabled me to prepare and sow my seeds on the same day. Without the help of this dry soil one could spend hours preparing and waiting for the bed to dry sufficiently to sow the seed. Often the sowing would have to be left over till the next day and thus run the risk of rain falling during the night, postponing the sowing for perhaps another week. I found another use for old soot which is worthy of note. Very early in the morning when the dew is on the ground it is comparatively easy to observe the little seedlings pushing through the soil, but it is most difficult if not impossible to see them clearly during bright sunlight. I discovered that by marking out the rows with soot I was able to use the hoe, when it became necessary, much more easily, and pushing it in front of me I was able to carry out the task almost as fast as I could walk. A useful idea when sowing onion seed is to sow a few seed of radishes in the same drill. The radishes will germinate much sooner than the onions making it possible to hoe the bed before the onion seedlings appear above the surface of the soil.

By the end of 1943 my stock of loam was almost exhausted and so I decided to use the turf from the grass paths in the kitchen garden. I dug up the paths dividing the garden across the centre and also grubbed out the fruit trees growing on either side. As well as solving my loam problem I gained valuable ground in which to grow vegetables. The following year I dug up a one hundred yard long path which separated the pear and plum trees growing against the wall facing west from the main garden and substituted a narrow dirt path.

I had and still possess a good supply of clay pots of all sizes, although these days they are fast disappearing from the garden scene. This is partly due to the labour cost of washing them. Although the modern cardboard pots filled with peat last only one season they are labour saving and have become very popular and so soon the potter's craft will have disappeared altogether. At Aynhoe, even to-day, we still have pots that date back to the 19th century, preserved by a clip over the ear for carelessness, also a lost tradition. The largest size pot I use today is a fourteen-inch, and it is still possible to buy a few of these. A nurseryman in Banbury tells me he still has a few in stock. It is however very doubtful if he will be able to obtain further supplies as he has been informed that there are only two old craftsmen remaining who are engaged in making these large pots, and when they retire no more will be made.

There was a ready market for all the foodstuff I was able to grow. I sold the produce direct to the public from the gardens, and for this purpose the gardens were opened from 6 p.m. until 7.30 p.m. on two evenings each week during the summer months and we had nearly always sold out by the time 7.30 arrived.

The fruit and vegetables were gathered and weighed during the afternoons, and by 5 p.m. queues began to form outside the garden, people coming from surrounding villages and some from as far away as Banbury, a distance of seven miles. The main attraction was the tomatoes, which were eagerly sought after to help supplement rations. The demand was so great that each person was allowed a pound of tomatoes only, in order that they could go right round. However the first in the queue were also allowed to purchase a pound of inferior tomatoes for cooking. Customers shopping at the Banbury green-grocers during this time were frequently limited to only one quarter of a pound of tomatoes at one time. I recall that somehow I always managed to serve each of my customers with a pound of tomatoes, and in order to achieve this I frequently revisited my plants several times each evening before the end of the queue was reached.

Following the outbreak of war, the army commandeered part of the Park House, and large parts of the pleasure grounds and adjacent park land, and thus I found another market for my produce, supplying fruit and vegetables to the officers' and sergeants' messes whenever possible. In addition I often supplied boxes of fruit to soldiers who were going home on leave, and these were made up of grapes, peaches, nectarines, various coloured plums, as well as apples, pears, and tomatoes. I was assured that these parcels were most welcome, and I received many repeat orders.

During these days, my working day began at 7 a.m. immediately after I had listened to the news on the radio, and ended just before 9 p.m., in time to hear the last news bulletin. This strict time-table was interrupted only when Home Guard duties intervened.

Just before the second summer of the war I was fortunate enough to obtain the regular services of a girl in her late teens who was very interested in gardening. She was a well-built girl and as strong as the average man, and during these difficult times she became invaluable to me. The demand for food was increasing now, and therefore I was obliged to dispense with such luxuries as asparagus and strawberries, in order that more potatoes and other essential vegetables might be grown, and although I was still tending the pleasure grounds they began inevitably to deteriorate, as I was able to devote less time to their care. The lawns, which we were forced to mow with ordinary machines, there being no fuel for the motor mowers, were also neglected, and finally only the grass immediately adjacent to the Park House was regularly cut. The rest was cut with scythes twice a year.

To make matters worse, the military were constantly erecting new buildings, and expanding their installations. Fruit trees were felled to make way for nissen huts, flower borders and box hedges were swept away, and cook houses and petrol dumps took their place. The outer kitchen garden was commandeered by the army, and was staffed by military gardeners to provide vegetables for their own cookhouses. Meanwhile, the long lean-to greenhouse situated on the outer wall at the bottom of the gardens, and in which I grew peaches, nectarines and tomatoes, was continually being broken into by military personnel, who obviously found that the proximity of the ripening fruit was too much of a temptation. Consequently, I cut out the trees and asked the military authorities if they would be prepared to take this greenhouse over. They agreed that this appeared to be the most practical solution, and thus they grew their own tomatoes, and thereafter a sentry was posted on the greenhouse whenever the fruit was ripening.

It was not until two years after the war that the army finally left Aynhoe Park, and although this quiet part of Northamptonshire had been far removed from the world's battlegrounds it had not entirely escaped the ravages of war; the surrounding park land pock-marked with abandoned concrete emplacements, empty nissen huts, petrol stores, and mourning still the many proud trees, and spacious lawns and rose gardens, which had been sacrificed as part of the contribution towards world peace. We had entered into a new era, and like so many of the stately homes and large country estates, Aynhoe Park would never be the same again. However, in 1947, I handed back the gardens to Mr. Cartwright, and the task of rebuilding began.

This entailed taking on extra labour and we immediately began collecting numerous concrete slabs left behind throughout the Estate by the army. The slabs were two feet square and two inches thick and had formed the bases of the petrol stores interspersed beneath the trees on the Estate which had provided natural camouflage. The slabs were extremely useful, and they had a certain amount of granite mixed with the cement which gave them a natural weathered appearance. A number of shrubs had been damaged and temporary paths had been hacked out amongst them, and so we decided to remove what had now become an eyesore, and to erect a terrace in its place. Shrubs which had formed the curtilage of the parklands had also been neglected and become misshapen and they were replaced by a low wall. Broken slabs were used to build the walls and whole slabs were used as coping stones and provided a neat finish to the construction work.

The box hedges surrounding the flower beds near the Park House had become so badly damaged that Mr. Cartwright decided that they should be swept away completely and I substituted a simple design of eight beds, each to be enclosed with new box hedges. Once again the slabs were utilised and provided neat paths between the flower beds. I used four slabs to form the base for a small sundial and this provided the centrepiece for the flower beds. The plot was divided into eight triangular beds with a two-foot slab path running between them and also around the outside of the beds.

After the main paths in the park had been regravelled the grounds began to look presentable again. The next problem to be tackled was the lawns. Fortunately the smaller lawns adjacent to the house had been kept mown with the aid of a hand mower, but the larger areas in front and away from the house had been allowed to grow wild and required a great deal of attention. The grass was initially cut with an Allen motor scythe and then rolled with a heavy roller before an attempt was made to use a motor mower. The following year we applied fertilisers and selective weed killers, and at last the lawns began to take on a fresh appearance, and the ravages of the war years were slowly repaired.

The greenhouses also required urgent renovation but before this could be undertaken they sustained further damage during some violent gales in the late spring of 1947 following which they looked so derelict that Mr. Cartwright suggested pulling them all down, and building two new plant houses which would be just sufficient to supply the necessary pot plants for the house. This meant that the vineries and peach houses which had over the years become almost my second home would have to be dismantled and the site levelled. I felt however that the damage appeared to be far worse than it actually was. A careful inspection revealed that the foundations and main rafters were perfectly sound, and so I persuaded Mr. Cartwright to allow me the sum of £50 to use in an effort to save the old houses. Thankfully my judgement proved right, for even as I write this chapter orchids are growing in one of these old houses. The long peach house at the bottom of the garden which had been taken over by the army towards the end of the war had suffered the worst damage. The majority of the glass had been broken and some of the ventilators torn away. The house was indeed beyond repair but it supplied me with valuable materials with which to repair the others. After the necessary repairs had been carried out I was still left with a considerable amount of material and with a second grant of £50 I was able to build a house with a span roof on the brick foundation of a large heated frame, and this compensated for the loss of the peach house.

Reluctantly many of the pre-war practices in the kitchen garden had to be abandoned for labour saving reasons. One major change was the use of a motor plough and cultivators instead of spade and rake. The many varied fruit trees trained along the garden walls, which for over a hundred years had provided an abundance of succulent fruit, were torn out of the ground, for no better reason than shortage of labour to attend to their many needs. The war years had certainly hastened the end of the old methods of cultivating and running a garden.

CHAPTER SEVENTEEN

Back to the Hall Again

IN NOVEMBER 1948, I WAS ABLE ONCE MORE TO EX-
hibit at the Royal Horticultural Society Hall, in London,
and whilst presenting my three cattleya plants, I decided
also to exhibit a seedling of zonal pelargonium, or as it is
commonly known, geranium. I was not surprised that this
seedling did not receive an award, but the following week
I received a letter from the Floral Committee of the R.H.S.
informing me that they would very much like the opportunity of seeing this variety again at a later date when it could
be shown bearing a larger number of flowers. Had it not
been for this letter I would never have bothered to show the
plant again, particularly since as far as I knew, no pelargonium had ever received an Award of Merit. Furthermore,
during the immediate post war years, pelargoniums had
lost their popularity in this country.

It was not until September 1950 that I had the opportunity of exhibiting the geranium, which I had named Elizabeth

165

Cartwright, at the R.H.S. Hall. I was travelling to London by train on private business, and decided to take the plant along with me. During the journey, I noticed that a few petals had fallen from the plant, and having the carriage to myself, I decided to unpack it, resolving that if too many petals had fallen I would not bother to show the plant, but would leave it in the cloakroom at Paddington Station until I had concluded my business. Fortunately, the plant was not too badly damaged, and I decided that I would exhibit it after all. I was delighted therefore when the plant was awarded an Award of Merit, receiving twenty votes for, and none against, from the Floral Committee, who described it as *a very distinct and beautiful greenhouse and bedding variety, with numerous large trusses of carmine-red single flowers measuring 2¼ inches across, the small white eye at the centre of the flower being surrounded by a small area of signal red which blends into the main colour with pleasing effect.*

Pleased as I was with this most satisfactory result, an even greater honour was forthcoming. On 6th December 1950, Mr. Cartwright received a letter from the R.H.S. informing him that the President of the Council had awarded the Sanders Gold Medal to the zonal pelargonium Elizabeth Cartwright for the best new greenhouse plant of general utility shown to the Society during the year. Presenting the medal two months later, the late Lord Aberconway, who was then President of the Council, said 'I know there are some people who do not like geraniums, just as they do not like dogs, or other people do not like cats. On the other hand, the geranium is a fine plant, I grow as many as I can myself. It goes on blooming all the summer, and we thought this particular one, Elizabeth Cartwright, was a distinct break, and a most wonderful thing, which well deserved the Sanders Medal.'

Realising that I possessed a plant outside the usual run, I soon began to increase my stock, and I discovered that whilst this could easily be done by seed, the resultant seedlings, although similar to the parent, were of an inferior nature, and I regret to say that eventually many inferior plants of Elizabeth Cartwright got on to the market, as had previously been the case with Paul Crampel.

In the circumstances, I discarded all my seedlings after they had flowered once, and increased my stock with cuttings.

Some time afterwards I received a visit from Mr. Anthony Ayton, who is a well-known authority on pelargoniums, and who was to some degree responsible for the formation of the Geranium Society, and I eventually sold my surplus stock of Elizabeth Cartwright to him. In one of his articles appearing in the *Gardening Illustrated* Mr. Ayton wrote *I would go so far as to say that this is the greatest step forward since Paul Crampel. An Award of Merit in 1950, and the Sanders Gold Medal, are only two steps which have been taken to bring this fantastic geranium to public notice. The plant is now available to the public, and can be purchased for a few shillings each from most of the specialist firms. I have it from the distributors that requests for stock have been received from thirteen different countries.*

Xenia Field, in one of the national daily newspapers, wrote *Let's please keep an eye open for Elizabeth Cartwright, a newish superb geranium likely to be the best commercial introduction since Paul Crampel. Last year it cost £1, and this year it has fallen to 10/-. Let us hope as it becomes more abundant it will go on falling in price. Anyhow it is worth waiting for.*

I have never been able to establish definitely the history of Elizabeth Cartwright although I feel reasonably certain that it was a cross between Banbury Cross and either King Edward VII or an extremely good Henry Jacoby. Banbury Cross was raised by a very close friend of mine, Mr. Fred Rawlings, a Banbury nurseryman, and he informs me that Banbury Cross was produced from Crampels Master, a fine variety which was the result of a cross between Paul Crampel and West Brighton Gem.

There also appear to be conflicting reports on the history of Paul Crampel. Mr. D. P. Clifford in his book on pelargoniums states that Paul Crampel was introduced in 1893 by V. Lemoine of Nancy, France. Another story I have heard is that for two years Paul Crampel went round his nursery after his staff had gone home, nipping the buds out so no one would know what a splendid flaming scarlet he had, while he worked up a huge stock.

Mr. Cross writes on geraniums—*The most famous geranium of all times is undoubtedly Paul Crampel. Monsieur Crampel had a famous geranium nursery at Nancy, and developed the variety that bears his name, and introduced them to the market. This was in the year 1903. Plants were sold at £1 a time. Several English nurserymen bought the plants, built up stocks, and introduced them at Covent Garden, where the red Henry Jacoby was then the most popular variety.*

This last story of Paul Crampel may or may not be true, but one thing seems certain. The year 1903 must be wrong, and this is borne out by the following excerpts from Messrs. H. Cannell & Sons' *Floral Guide of Plants 1901.* which lists almost seven hundred varieties of pelargoniums:

> *Catalogue No. 364. Henry Jacoby Crimson, 6d. each or 3/6d per dozen.*
>
> *Catalogue No. 367. West Brighton Gem. An exceedingly free variety of bright scarlet colour, 4/- per dozen.*
>
> *Catalogue No. 365. Paul Crampel. A spendid brilliant variety, 1/- each, 10/- per dozen.*

Henry Jacoby, known more than eighty years ago, produced a sport, which was a novelty in 1901, named King Edward VII. Cannell's catalogue described it as *A new and improved Henry Jacoby with a light coloured flower stalk similar in this respect to West Brighton Gem. The flowers of this grand introduction are a lovely, dark velvety crimson that has been much appreciated in its parent, and forms a striking contrast. It has an excellent habit, and is effective as a pot plant.*

Fred Rawlings, whom I have already mentioned, and who has two Awards of Merit to his credit, tells a very different story on the origin of Paul Crampel. Apparently, when exhibiting his Banbury Cross geranium at the R.H.S. Hall, he came into conversation with a gentleman, whose name unfortunately he cannot recall, and the subject of the parentage of Paul Crampel was discussed. Mr. Rawlings's acquaintance informed him that Paul Crampel had been raised by a friend of his, who had subsequently worked up a stock, which he eventually sold. Some time later a traveller called upon the grower and requested him to retrieve the stocks that he had sold, as a Royal Personage had seen the geranium, and had expressed his wish that these fine plants should grace the flower beds in front of Buckingham Palace. Whether he was able to fulfil this task I cannot say.

I feel sure that many growers, who like myself experiment by crossing various kinds of plants, without ever dreaming of raising anything new or of special value, neglect to record accurately the varieties used in their experiments. I made this mistake, and therefore I would encourage any young grower to take the little time and trouble necessary to document the parentage of the crosses properly.

Encouraged by my success with Elizabeth Cartwright I decided in 1951 to exhibit a large specimen plant, a semi-double brick red seedling which I named Aynhoe Park, and which was awarded a Certificate of Cultural Commendation, and in February 1953 I exhibited a pure white seedling which I had named after myself, as I had always been fond of white flowers. This plant gained an Award of Merit, and was described in the R.H.S. report as *A pure white zonal pelargonium of great excellence, the individual flowers measuring two inches across, being of good shape and substance, and borne in a compact and well-rounded truss, held erect on a strong stem.* The *Gardener's Chronicle* described the plant as *A chastely beautiful pure white variety in which the rounded shapely petals are held flat and are very striking.*

It was approximately three and a half years later that I exhibited another seedling, a zonal pelargonium of unknown parentage, named Viscount Weir. This plant also gained an Award of Merit and was described as *A very distinct and beautiful addition to the zonal pelargoniums. The individual rose pink flowers with veining of a deeper shade are borne*

*in good bold trusses and measure from two to two and a half inches
across. They are freely produced and do not appear to lose their
petals prematurely, which is an important point, especially when
plants of this kind are used for bedding.*

In April 1958, I gained yet another Award of Merit, this
time for a regal pelargonium which I had named Eustace
Hoare. The R.H.S. report described the plant as being
*Obviously very free flowering, and capable of making a fine speci-
men plant with large heads of pure white flowers, bearing light
purple markings.*

In 1958 I raised an interesting plant which was a cross
between a zonal seedling and an ivy leaf seedling. This
plant produced large double flowers on a strong stem, very
similar to a zonal, but with the creeping habit of the ivy leaf.
I exhibited this plant too, and it received a Preliminary
Commendation. At about this time I had contemplated
working up a collection of pelargoniums to be known as
the Aynhoe Park strain, but circumstances prevented me
from increasing my stock and raising new varieties. However
I still possess a few plants of each of my successful strains.

Briefly, I will describe my method of cultivating geraniums.
Cuttings are taken in August or September, and planted
singly in small pots using a John Innes No. 1 or similar
mixture. When the cuttings have taken root, they should be
stopped to ensure bushy plants. Approximately three weeks
later the cuttings should be potted in three and a half inch-
pots in which they will stand the winter, being kept on the
dry side.

The plants should be re-potted in February into six-inch
pots, a John Innes No. 2 compost being used, and should
again be stopped. However any plants which are required
for early flowering should be allowed to grow on without
further check.

Plants for late or winter flowering should be stopped up
to the end of August whilst at no time previous to this
should any flowers be allowed to develop. When coming
into flower they need slight warmth, 45 to 50 degrees Fahrenheit as the minimum, with a free circulation of air to keep

down damp. These winter flowering plants do not require nearly so much water as those that flower earlier in the year. However, weak doses of artificial manure alternating weekly with cow manure in liquid form assists growing. Occasionally you should give weak soot water instead of cow manure. I remember some of the fine specimen plants grown at Aynhoe during the early 1920's. These plants grew in ten-inch pots with a dozen or more trusses of flowers on long strong stems above green healthy foliage. When potting them in their final pots, they were always potted low, as during winter when the plants were not receiving so much water, this meant that they did not get so much feed. Also room was left to give several small rich top dressings. I have found this method very helpful in growing all kinds of specimen plants.

With a little planning, geraniums, either with flowers or foliage, can be attractive throughout the year. They are valuable as pot plants, and if their potentialities are fully exploited they provide a colourful display of flowers from late spring until the end of the year. The commonest causes of poor results are overcrowding, loose potting and too much nitrogen.

With a little skill and care, geraniums can be grown into large specimens, but for the average cultivator, it is best to maintain fresh stock by taking cuttings each year.

Browsing through old catalogues and gardening journals has led me to believe that we can learn a good deal from the patience and skill exercised by the growers in the last century. This was especially so with Cannell's *Floral Guide* in which there is a wealth of information and advice.

The following extracts from Cannell's catalogue show that these nurseries were indeed invaluable to a great many young gardeners.

To Ladies and Gentlemen in Request of Gardeners.
Our Mr. H. Cannell Senr. gives personal daily attention to all applications for Gardeners (good all-round men). His wide connection, and being a large employer, makes him intimately acquainted with

*most of the best practical and deserving men in the country, and he
would feel a real pleasure in assisting and fitting in the right man
to fill the situation for which any lady or gentlemen may require him.*

On page 1 of the Guide is the following:—

Thirty-Fourth Edition
HENRY CANNELL & SONS.,
(F.R.H.S., M.S.A., M.R.A.S.,)
ILLUSTRATED FLORAL GUIDE FOR 1901

*All our catalogues as they are issued are known, acknowledged and
anxiously looked for throughout the entire gardening loving World as
the accepted printed organs for descriptions of all the choicest Flowers
Fruits and Vegetables. Editors ask for two or three copies, and
preserve them as historical references. We are further known by
ardent foreign amateurs and professionals as the most successful ex-
porters in England of both plants and seeds into the most distant
countries in the World. Our long experience shows that our pure
country grown plants and seeds not only grow stronger at home and
give the greatest satisfaction abroad, but survive the long journeys
better—so it is frequently written us—than others, while the modes
we adopt are considered marvellous, and bring us much eulogy from
New Zealand, Australia etc.*

It may be of interest to read of a few of the varieties of
plants grown in addition to pelargoniums, and the extent
of these famous nurseries of more than fifty years ago.

*Over 70 varieties of Carnations
1600 varieties of Chrysanthemums
1000 plants of Dahlias
180 varieties of Fuchias
67 varieties of Petunias
80 varieties of Phlox
10 acres of Roses, 5000 in pots.*

*Several acres of Hardy Perennials and Flowering Plants. A
large selection of Stove and Greenhouse Plants including 26 varieties
of Palms. A 150 foot house filled entirely with plants of the Cacti
family. A large variety of Orchids. A vast quantity of Strawberry*

Runners in small pots to fruit the first year. 12/- to 14/- per 100.
Special Prices per 1,000—50,000 and 100,000.
Quite a large private trade in cut flowers.
Orders for cut flowers from 2/6 upwards can be sent Letter or
Parcel Post.

I was extremely interested in the item on grapes—

Grape Vines are grown very extensively; four of our 100 ft.
houses are filled with them early in the spring, and afterwards (the
houses) used for drying seeds during August and September.
Each year we have some unsold from the preceeding year's sale,
carrying bunches of Grapes. These are of great importance when a
house is required to be filled at once. At all seasons these Vines if
planted intact and laid sideways together with two feet of stem, six
inches below the surface, will at once put forth young fresh roots,
make extra strong canes first season, and fruit at once.

And finally on the back page was an engraving with the
following words;

The above engraving gives an idea—but not nearly so elegant and
beautiful as it should—of our exhibit 30 feet long and 6 feet broad
composed of a most brilliant group of Cannas at each end—one side
of dazzling Zonal Pelargoniums, the other filled with the choicest,
newest and rarest Chrysanthemums. For years at our Show at the
Royal Aquarium we have had there similar flowers in great per-
fection although so late in the year. Commencing in October, again
at the big Show in November, and even so late as the December
Exhibition, our displays have been continued and their attractive-
ness maintained by saving the centre. In the Engraving above will
be noticed extraordinarily fine plants of Acalypha sanderi.
December it was filled with Begonia *Gloire de Lorraine 2 to 3 feet*
high, certainly the finest plants and flowers ever seen in London. On
each of the three occasions last year we were awarded the Large
Gold Medal while for over 20 years similar exhibits have secured
for us more Gold Medals than any other firm and what is more
remarkable in these days, every plant has been of our own growth
and production.
Sic transit gloria mundi.

CHAPTER EIGHTEEN
Open House

D URING THE EARLY 1950'S, AYNHOE PARK
House and the pleasure grounds were open to the
public, and once again I was required to provide
flowers to decorate the House, thus transforming it from
a museum or exhibition into the fine country residence
which it undoubtedly was.

Although Aynhoe House had now become one of the
dozens of half-crown houses which had opened up and
down the country, it remained a home, a home that was
lived in, and this was emphasised by the floral arrangements,
giving visitors the welcome that only flowers provide. The
secret of growing a plant for house decorating is to grow
a healthy plant in a small pot with good foliage, and a large
head of flowers.

Azaleas, one of the plants we grew, are extremely valuable
as house plants, lasting in bloom over a long period. Hundreds of thousands are grown and distributed annually.

Azaleas may be placed out of doors from the end of June to the beginning of September. To prevent them being blown over by the wind, plunge them in a border that is shaded from the midday sun. Just to dig a hole and sink the pot in would probably mean the plant would become water-logged and possibly full of worms. The correct method is to dig a hole much deeper than the pot and half fill it with coarse gravel, putting a small piece of slate where you intend to stand the pot, to prevent worms entering the compost. Before standing the pot on the slate, put several pieces of wood, match-sticks would do, to lift the pot slightly to allow the water to drain away from the plant. Another idea is to plunge the pots up to the rim in a bed of coarse gravel. Camellia, hydrangeas, rhododendrons, and roses in pots, can all be treated this way. Another valuable plant for decorative purposes is *Ophiopogon jaburan* which was grown very freely for the markets in the late 1800's. It is a Japanese plant with narrow strap-like leaves, longitudinally banded with white, creamy or yellow bands, and white flowers. Apart from its leaves I think its greatest attraction is the colour of its berries, which are purple with a beautiful bloom, similar to that of the grape.

I had not seen this plant for many years until a few months ago when I visited an old gardening friend of mine. He had three plants and thought the plant was very rare to-day, so that he was hoping to grow a nice specimen plant with a view to showing it in the R.H.S. Hall. He kindly gave me a small division which is now growing away nicely. I am sure this would be a valuable plant for bottle gardening, which is so popular to-day. There was another known variety called *Japonica*, also variagated, with broader leaves, and lilac flowers.

Clivias with their strap shaped leaves and their large umbels of showy flowers in various shades of orange-red well above the leaves are also fine house plants, and another is *Begonia* Gloire de Lorraine. If you continually pick off fading flowers and apply a weekly dose of liquid manure, this latter plant will remain in bloom over a long period.

The present day Lorraines have a sturdier habit and larger flowers than their predecessors which had a more graceful habit with a wealth of blooms. In my opinion I doubt if one could now grow the wonderful specimens seen in the early 1900's. Another begonia we grew in those days and one I would like to have again is *Begonia* Gloire de Sceaux. Being quite distinct from the Lorraine group, it had a beautiful bronze foliage of perfect shape which showed to advantage the panicles of rosy pink flowers.

The month of March was always a busy month for me, preparations for the official opening on April 1st being in full swing, and the month of March 1954 was no exception.

Little did we think that a great tragedy was imminent, a tragedy which was to effect the future of Aynhoe Park, and the lives of all of us closely connected with the Cartwright family. On the evening of March 30th Mr. Cartwright and his only son Edward, who was then aged seventeen years, were both killed instantaneously in a motor-car accident, almost within sight of Aynhoe, as they were returning home from London.

The ensuing days were very sad ones indeed, and I was kept busy helping to make some of the many beautiful floral tributes for the funeral. I had the honour of being selected as one of the bearers, and thus I helped carry Mr. Cartwright, my friend as well as my employer, to his last resting place.

Several days after the funeral, Mrs. Cartwright informed me that she would continue to manage the Estate until her daughter Elizabeth became of age five years hence, when she would automatically inherit the Estate. The next year Miss Elizabeth and her mother moved from the Park House, and took up residence in the nearby Dower House, which had been let on lease since 1916, and had become sadly neglected. This house was known as Friars Well, so called because of the well in its grounds from which monks had drawn water for use at their Friary close by. This meant of course that I now had another house and garden to supply, the Park House now only being used for special functions such as dinner parties, except of course when it was officially opened to the public.

In the autumn of 1955 a start was made to rejuvenate the garden at Friars Well and the first task was to have a general clean up. Trees and shrubs that had been allowed to grow wild were to be grubbed out. Once the wild neglected parts of the garden were clean, grass seed could be sown, and beds, borders and paths made later. All the branches of the trees to be grubbed out were cut off and burnt, leaving the main stems. A trench two to three feet from the base of the trees and two feet deep was dug around each tree, severing all roots as the work proceeded. Using the main stem as a lever the trees were pulled up by their roots by the farm tractor. The shrubs were also lifted out with their roots in the same manner, except that an iron bar with its end resting on a flat stone was used to lever them out of the ground. The holes left after the trees and shrubs had been cleared away were partly filled in with the stones lying about, and finally filled in by digging around each hole in a circle. This operation also roughly levelled the ground. The next task was to cultivate and level ready for sowing the grass seed. This we did using a small garden tractor and cultivators. The cultivators were fixed to penetrate the soil to a depth of three inches, and by fixing a three sided box without top or bottom on to the tool bar at ground level, we were able to cultivate and level at the same time. The next tasks were to rebuild walls, make terraces, and re-surface existing paths. The stone to carry out these tasks came from an old dovecote standing nearby. Unfortunately this old dovecote, another relic of the past, had been sadly neglected. The timber was rotten and the roof caving in, and in fact the building was in a dangerous condition, so reluctantly the decision was made to pull it down. The eighteen-inch thick walls of this old dovecote were of stone, except the inside of the gables. These were of brick, one of which protruded half its length every square foot to provide resting places for the birds. A modern swimming pool now occupies the site where the old dovecote stood.

In May 1957, Mrs. Cartwright gave a coming out dance for Miss Elizabeth at the the Park House. Much of the furniture in the House was removed for this event, being loaded into large vans which were hidden away for the night among the trees bordering the Lime Avenue. This secret was so well kept that even I did not know until Miss Elizabeth told me when compiling notes for this book.

The floral arrangements inside the house were carried out by Lady Rose McLaren who ran an organisation known as Floral Services Ltd. Very few pot plants were required, although I did provide a number, amongst which were some particularly fine specimens of Canterbury bell (cup and saucer variety). Huge banks of flowers and foliage were artistically arranged, and I especially admired those that included yellow arum lilies. On the dinner table a number of small vases of stephanotis and yellow rose buds blended perfectly with the gold centrepiece and silver gilt candlesticks. To add to all this beauty, electric light bulbs shed a soft subdued light on the old and beautiful paintings that graced the walls of the main rooms and staircases.

I was, however, responsible for the floral arrangements outside the house, and the main display was provided by the eight flower beds on the west side of the house. Each bed was triangular in shape, and a small sundial formed the centrepiece. The flower beds which were edged with box contained a thousand antirrhinums and a thousand nemesias, and provided a splendid mass of colour for the occasion. Across the lawn from the flower beds was a paved terrace, which was situated between two fine beech trees, and on this terrace a wooden platform was erected in order that the younger guests might enjoy themselves in their own fashion without intruding on their more sedate parents, a small band being engaged to provide the necessary rock and roll music for them to dance to. The platform provided for the dancing did not appear unseemly and blended into the beautiful surroundings, the edges of the platform being covered with moss, with small pots of coleus, nemesia, geraniums, marigolds and ferns buried amongst it.

The bases of the trees were similarly decorated, and on the terrace stood specially grown coleus, Canterbury bells, geraniums, stocks, hydrangeas and ferns, and boxes of these same plants graced the terrace steps. The terrace was illuminated by coloured lights, and special features in the pleasure grounds were floodlit, and as though in approval of all these preparations the weather was kind. It was a fine clear summer's evening, and the whole effect was very beautiful, and was a reward in itself for those of us who had helped to create it.

The one thing that the pleasure grounds at the Park House lacked was water. Even without the addition of plants, water can add charm to the garden, introducing an entirely different contrasting landscape to the existing lawns and borders. To the south-west of the House on a gradual slope there was an ideal site for a lake, a natural basin approximately seventy-five yards long, fifty yards wide and from ten to fifteen feet deep in the centre. This area was in an open position with a path and low wall on one side and the old Yew Mound on the other.

Even had there been no natural springs, and I had every reason to assume there would be, water to fill this basin could come from the rain falling on the roof of the house. This volume of rain water could easily be directed over a few water falls into the lake, the overflow, if any, draining away down the park. Quantities of clay were available to line the sides and bottom, also large weathered rocks to form the series of water falls. Miss Elizabeth was very enthusiastic with the idea but before a start could be made the House and grounds were sold.

Aynhoe Park was taken over by the Mutual Housing Association in 1959 and my connections with the House and grounds finally severed. I felt a little sad about this after nearly fifty years but I am pleased to say the grounds are nicely kept up, so different from some of the Mutual Homes where the sharers do the gardening.

What so often happens then when everyone has an area to attend, is that someone goes on holiday and the others poach, as there is no-one in command. For a garden to be run successfully it can only have one head gardener, as a ship has only one captain. I understand that at Aynhoe all the sharers contribute towards the upkeep of the garden, and have a gardening committee with the chairman in charge. This I think is an excellent idea, and one to be recommended.

CHAPTER NINETEEN
Orchids at Aynhoe

CONTRARY TO GENERAL BELIEF, MOST ORCHIDS are not difficult to cultivate, and indeed certain species are easier to grow than other more common plants. Orchids are easily kept free of insects and plant diseases, and they require only occasional watering.

Orchids can be taken into the home, and when positioned to advantage they will enhance and grace any room. As for temperature, whilst the plant is in your home it is generally accepted that if you are comfortable yourself your plant will be also. After the plant has been in the home for about a month it should be returned to the growing area, but remember that orchid blooms usually last from four to eight weeks, and therefore you can cut them from the plant and place them in a vase where they can continue to add their decorative charm to your home.

As I have already mentioned, one of the most beautiful of the orchid family is the cattleya, and there are some varieties of this type of orchid which can be grown in the home, as can some of the cypripediums (Slipper orchids). Fifty years ago specimen plants of *Cypripedium insigne*, with their green leaves encircling the pot so closely that one saw a bank of foliage without a gap, and rising above the foliage fifty to a hundred blooms, apple green, speckled with brown and tipped with white in colour, formed one of the leading features in the greenhouse, and for house decoration.

They are comparatively easy to grow and their flowers will keep in perfect condition for many weeks during the dull months of the year, for the cost of only a few shillings per plant.

Although it is nearly a hundred and fifty years since they were first grown in this country they must still be widely grown judging by the large number of flowers sold by the florists each year. I would advise anyone just starting to grow cypripediums for the first time, to start with the *insigne* type. For cultural purposes cypripediums are usually divided into two groups; those with plain leaves like the *insigne* which will grow and flower in a cool greenhouse, and the mottled leaf varieties and their hybrids which require warmer conditions. Temperatures for these should not fall below 60 to 65 degrees Fahrenheit at night.

I think the most interesting task of the whole year is that of tying the flowers to a thin bamboo cane and this operation is best carried out when the flowers are in a fairly advanced bud stage. Some varieties have strong sturdy stems and need no support, but those with thinner stems and fairly large blooms, if neglected or overlooked, will never hold themselves erect, resulting in bent stems and twisted flowers.

February and March are probably the best months to see cypripediums in flower, and they are also the months when one should think about potting and dividing the plants, preparing the compost, seeing that a number of pots of different sizes are thoroughly clean and breaking up cracked pots into small pieces, which together with dirty crocks can be washed and put into two sizes by shaking through a sieve and stored ready for use.

Whether one is growing cattleyas, cymbidiums or cypripediums the task of potting and dividing is very similar. Personally I believe in early and annual potting of·all warm house varieties of cypripediums, using as small a pot as will accommodate the roots without cramping them into a ball or damaging them in any way. Cypripediums are lazy in making roots, depending largely on their leaves to draw what substance they can from the atmosphere, so you should not be surprised if a healthy plant has only a scanty root system. Warmth and moisture are therefore very necessary and to help maintain moisture in the atmosphere stand the plants on an inverted pot or a wooded slatted stage placed upon a staging of corrugated sheets covered with gravel. It is surprising how much moisture is maintained in the gravel and valleys of the corrugated sheets.

Before re-potting, the compost should be moderately moist and if the pot was perfectly clean before use the plant should leave the pot without damage to the roots. Most of the old compost should be carefully prised away, and any dead or decaying roots cut back to their point of issue or until a live healthy part is reached. Before I begin to re-pot I always have a small jar of powdered sulphur standing by, and I plunge the blade of the knife I am using in the jar. I also dust the cut roots with a brush dipped in a little sulphur. The plant is now ready either for potting or dividing. If the plant has only one old flower growth and one new growth it should be re-potted. If on the other hand the plant has two or more old flowers and new growth it can be divided. During August and September the roots are very active and the plants must receive sufficient water at the root to keep the compost moist at all times, as failure to do this often results in deformed flowers and weak sickly-looking plants. During October very little shade will be needed and as the sunlight declines, this should be dispensed with altogether until the early spring months when shade must once again be provided.

An orchid valuable for table decoration, or as a pot plant buried in ferns during the early months of the year, is the deciduous calanthe. They are easily grown in a warm humid atmosphere with a minimum temperature of 65 degrees Fahrenheit during the growing season. Most varieties start into growth in March or April and must be re-potted before the new roots are very far advanced. The old compost is shaken out from the roots which are cut off to one inch from the pseudo bulbs to help hold the bulbs in position until the new roots are well established. I also leave on one foot of the old flower stalk. My method of re-potting is as follows. First, using clean six-inch pots, I hold a cane in position and half fill a pot with crocks and then, using a compost of equal parts of loam with all the fine particles teased out, coarse peat, chopped sphagnum moss and dried cow manure, with an addition of charcoal and silver sand to keep the compost porous, I fill the pot and lightly firm to about one inch from the top. The bulbs are tied by the old flower stalks to the cane, and the roots, but not the young growths, carefully covered with compost.

No water is necessary until the new growths are developing freely, but the surroundings must be kept moist by frequent syringings. To help keep the compost moist I place pieces of broken pot around the bulbs, removing them as the growths expand.

The cymbidium is undoubtedly the toughest of the orchid family, and will grow in a lower temperature than other varieties. It will also produce a larger number of flowers during its life if it is properly tended. Actually it is the easiest orchid to grow, and therefore the following hints will be of some interest to the amateur grower who wishes to embark on the cultivation of orchids. It should always be borne in mind that one of the most difficult and important tasks in growing any plant is correct watering, and this can only be mastered by experience.

The roots of the cymbidium are large and fleshy, and are without root hairs, and therefore they require a generous supply of air to keep them healthy, hence the use of a compost that allows water to pass through freely. Cymbidiums store water in their roots, and to a lesser extent in their leaves. The active root tip sucks up the water, and therefore if the roots of the plant are dormant, an excess of water will only make the roots rot. If in doubt it is advisable to discontinue watering for a day or two, and concentrate on applying a liberal foliage spray, using tepid rain water.

It is well to remember that whilst good clean rain water in the country is undoubtedly the best, in large towns it is likely to become polluted with sulphuric impurities from the atmosphere, and so could be far more harmful to the plant than the average tap water. In this event it is advisable to keep a supply of tap water in the greenhouse at least a week before it is likely to be required. Where a plant is really suffering for lack of water, the bulb will begin to shrivel.

The most beneficial form of watering, especially during the winter months, is best effected by dipping the plants in a bucket of water. Once a week is usually enough from October to May, although during the month of December and January once a fortnight should be sufficient. I advise this method of watering every week rather than from a can, because by handling each individual plant every week it affords an opportunity of inspecting it for possible overwatering, and for such pests as slugs and red spider.

The red spider mites are the most damaging of all orchid pests. They seldom appear on the upper side of the leaves, preferring the softer tissue and shelter offered by the underside, and therefore unless plants are examined periodically, their presence may not be noticed until they have caused considerable damage. No larger than a pin head, they are bright red in colour, although occasionally they are colourless. If allowed to remain, the red spider will pierce the plant cells, removing the sap and chlorophyll. If not detected their numbers increase at an alarming pace, and as a result the foliage on the plant will become yellow and spotted. The red spider is also the main distributor of plant viruses.

When the time comes for re-potting the cymbidium, I like to prepare two heaps of compost, one for the bottom half of the pot and one for the top. When preparing the sphagnum moss I take off the top live green inch for use in the top layer of compost, the remainder being used in the bottom layer.

Having ensured that the pot is clean, a few broken crocks are placed in an upright position in the bottom of the pot. This ensures that the drainage hole does not become blocked, for this could easily happen if a flat crock was placed over the hole. A layer of smaller crocks are then placed over the upright ones to a depth of approximately one inch. Then follows a layer of coarse osmunda fibre which serves the purpose of preventing the finer materials from falling between the crocks and thus blocking the drainage.

The plant should be placed in the pot so that the leading growth is as near to the centre as possible, and the pot selected should be large enough to allow a space of two inches all around the plant, except where the back bulb touches the edge of the pot.

The compost used should consist of two parts osmunda fibre, washed and cut into pieces approximately two inches square, and one part sphagnum moss. To each two-gallon bucketful of this mixture, one pint each of broken charcoal and broken clay brick are added, together with a sprinkling of coarse silver sand.

A handful of the prepared compost is placed around the plant and made firm, at the same time is added a small quantity of coarse bonemeal, a heaped teaspoonful to a six-inch pot being sufficient. This operation is continued until the pot is three-quarters filled. The second pile of compost, consisting of two parts osmunda fibre and one part live green sphagnum moss with a liberal sprinkling of charcoal and silver sand, is then used. When the pot has been completely filled it should be neatly trimmed off with a pair of scissors.

Light intensity is an important factor in the production of flower spikes, as even a slight film of dirt on the glass can cause up to ten per cent loss of light, and therefore the necessity of washing the glass of the greenhouse during autumn and winter cannot be over emphasised.

Cymbidiums have of course to be protected from bright sunlight, and cotton blinds which can be raised and lowered as required will afford the best protection. They are however, rather expensive, and the most usual substitute is Green Summer Cloud applied thickly on the glass. From about the second week in June until the third week in September the plants can stand outside, this being more beneficial than being kept in a small stuffy greenhouse. If this plan is implemented, a sheltered position receiving full sunlight should be chosen. A polythene cover fitted about two feet above the plants will protect them from the midday sun, and if a cold frame is available in which to stand the plants so much the better, for the sides of the frame will give protection against the wind.

Alternatively the pots can be buried to about half their depth, care being taken to ensure that the drainage hole is not blocked. The plants will still require to be dipped in water once each week, and once every fortnight, the day following the weekly dip, they should be sprayed with a weak solution of Clay's fertiliser, one level teaspoonful to each gallon of water being sufficient. During hot dry spells, the plants require spraying three or four times during the day, both the top and underside of the leaves being so treated. At other times the rainfall is quite sufficient.

When the flower spikes begin to appear, any attempt to hurry them into bloom generally results in bud dropping, and even those that do flower will not compare favourably with those allowed to grow naturally. Other dangers at this time are the presence of slugs and thrips, although with the present-day methods of destroying pests these do not present difficult problems provided one is vigilant.

Another orchid that will flourish in a cymbidium house or even at a kitchen window is *Coelogyne cristata*. However, if they are allowed a winter temperature of 55 degrees Fahrenheit they will respond even better. They require abundant supplies of water whilst growing, but must have a decided rest during the latter part of November and during December, and water should be withheld during these months.

The blooms are white with a yellow base to the lip, and have a delightful delicate scent. A plant was dispatched to me from Scotland about ten years ago, and unfortunately owing to delay on the railway services and a severe spell of weather during transit it reached me in a sorry state, and seemed unlikely to survive. However, I broke the plant up and persuaded several shoots to grow, and these have now grown together into one large plant. In February 1965 it carried 125 blooms on 23 spikes and was awarded a Certificate of Cultural Commendation by the Orchid Committee of the Royal Society, who described it as a superb specimen.

This story of *Coelogyne cristata*, and earlier references contained in earlier chapters, illustrate that the orchid is not the delicate plant so many people imagine it to be, the majority of orchids in fact possessing tough and lasting qualities.

During severe weather, one often encounters the difficulty of maintaining a correct temperature, and during these times, if watering and damping between plants is restricted to the minimum, the plants, although they may receive a slight check from the lower temperatures, will soon recover when normal conditions are resumed. On the other hand if the plants and their surrounding are kept wet, serious trouble may result which will not become apparent until several weeks later.

In June 1957, having a large specimen plant of *Laeliocattleya eximia* in bloom I exhibited it before the R.H.S. Orchid Committee, and was awarded a Certificate of Cultural Commendation for the plant. The blooms graduated from pale rose to deep purple, and were most striking. The reader may well wonder why I concentrated on growing these large specimen plants. In fact there were a number of reasons. Firstly, no matter what variety of plants are grown, it is the large specimen plant which is most admired, and furthermore I have always felt that the production of such a plant is a challenge to one's skill as a grower. Then, as I was always required to decorate large rooms, this type of plant became a necessity, and finally, bearing in mind that the R.H.S. award Certificates of Cultural Commendation for special cultural skill, the production of specimen plants increases the likelihood of gaining this award.

The production of a specimen plant is not easy. In the first place, it is necessary to select the right type of plant, in other words, one which possesses free growing and free flowering qualities. Having selected a suitable plant it becomes a challenge to the grower's skill and patience, since large plants are not produced in one or two seasons, and with orchids it may take years. As soon as the selected plant produces more than the average number of blooms, the grower will experience the immense satisfaction that is derived from the specialised cultivation, and from this stage the recipe for success will depend on special consideration being given to re-potting, compost and watering.

Whilst on the subject of specimen plants, I feel I must dwell for a short while on the one which has given me the greatest satisfaction, namely *Brassocattleya* Viscountess Weir which I have tended for the past 20 years. In March 1958 I was awarded a Certificate of Cultural Commendation for this plant by the R.H.S. Orchid Committee, for what was described as a *magnificent specimen*. The plant then growing in an eight-inch pot carried ten perfect blooms. In March 1965 I again showed this plant and received yet another Certificate of Cultural Commendation by the R.H.S. Orchid Committee for what was described as *A magnificent plant*, the report in the *Orchid Review* being:—*This mammoth-sized plant, undivided since raised from seed, and contained in an eighteen-inch diameter pan, carried thirty-six large white flowers, flushed with mauve, and with a white throat.* On the first occasion that this plant bloomed it carried one flower only, and thereafter it grew in a practically straight line, the leading growths becoming a little larger in each succeeding year. The only time that this increase was not noticeable was after I had cut through the rhizome to encourage the plant to make new growth.

The reader will have gathered from my previous reference to the *American Orchid Review*, and to correspondence that I have had with American citizens, that there is a wide interest in orchids in that country, and thanks to the world renowned travel agents Messrs. Thos. Cook & Son, who in 1958 arranged a series of tours from the United States and Canada, entitled *Cook's Human Interest Tours of Europe*, I experienced the pleasure of visits from a number of Americans who showed great interest in the orchids at Aynhoe. I for my part thoroughly enjoyed their company, and was able to exchange some useful information with them on the subject of orchids.

Quoting from the brochure of this forty-two day tour, which commenced with five days in London and the English countryside:— *On the morning of the fourth day, after a drive through gently rolling countryside, you will arrive at Aynhoe Park, a gracious English manor house that has been in the Cartwright family since 1616. Aynhoe Park contains an infinite variety of priceless furniture, Chinese porcelain, paintings and objets d'art. Its great park stretching for many acres makes a perfect setting for the house.*

You will visit the Head Gardener, Mr. Humphris, and see his world famous orchid plant. At lunch in the Cartwright Arms, the local pub, you will meet some of the villagers who will show you round this friendly and peaceful corner of England.

Earlier in this chapter I wrote that one of the most difficult and important tasks in growing any plant is correct watering. The following six points may be of help:—

1. Normally a heavy soil holds water better than an open or light soil containing a large proportion of coarse particles like sand. Under ideal conditions, the water is present around the particles, with air in the tiny spaces between, so that the roots may breathe. Too close a texture or too much water drives the air from these spaces with the result that the roots are more or less suffocated.

2. Plants with thick, leathery, wavy or hairy leaves require less water than a plant with large thin leaves.

3. A plant with a large leaf surface in a small pot will require more water than a plant with a smaller leaf surface.

4. When a plant has taken possession of all the soil in the pot, a condition referred to as pot-bound, the plant will require more water to keep it healthy.

5. A plant in active or full growth will require more water than one at rest.

6. Plants in a moist, still atmosphere will use up less water than those in a dry, moving atmosphere.

CHAPTER TWENTY
More Changes at Aynhoe

IN NOVEMBER 1957, ANOTHER GREAT CHANGE took place, the marriage between the Hon. Mrs. Cartwright and Mr. Eustace Hoare of South Street, London. From 1959 I was required to take charge of the floral decorations at Mr. & Mrs. Hoare's town house. There was a small ornamental garden there, which had been constructed in the area at the rear of the house. This garden was, I understand, designed by Lutyens. On one special occasion a temporary roof was erected there, from which suspended three chandeliers. The walls were draped with green silk, and electric heating was installed. In addition to the flower beds and window boxes, all of which were freshly planted, I arranged large groups of flowers including such favourites as arum lilies, schyzanthus, pelargoniums, Canterbury bells, and foliage plants such as aphelandras, coleus, and ferns. The whole effect beneath the artificial lighting was truly enchanting, and it was hard to believe that one was merely a

few yards from the chaos of the never-ending London
traffic.

The aphelandra has recently become an exceedingly
popular house plant. Its cockade of brilliant yellow bracts
makes a striking contrast with its dark green foliage which
is marked with white veins. Often it is found difficult to
grow in the house, and this is hardly surprising when one
realises that it is a native of the West Indies. This being so,
it will only prosper when it is kept warm, and it requires a
night temperature of 55 to 60 degrees Fahrenheit in winter
with a correspondingly higher temperature in spring and
summer. When in full growth, the plant requires a moist
atmosphere, and only when the flowers fade and the plant is
half resting will it tolerate a dry atmosphere.

A plant which has been subjected to a dry atmosphere for
a long period sometimes loses some of its lower leaves. If
this should happen, it is possible to reduce the height of the
plant by encouraging new roots to sprout at a convenient
point higher up the stem. This is effected by making a
slanting cut half way through the stem, making sure to use a
sharp knife. The cut is then dressed with a liberal amount of
rooting powder, Seradix B, after which a pad of sphagnum
moss can be applied and bound with polythene to ensure
that the operation is air-tight.

The roots will soon begin to form, and eventually they
will penetrate the moss. When this happens, the polythene
binding should be removed, and the mass of roots covered
by a prepared compost. This operation is effected by cutting
a paper pot containing the prepared compost in half, and
placing the two halves around the roots, making the pot
secure at the same time. In other words the new plant is
potted whilst still on the main stem. About a fortnight later
a further incision should be made half way through the main
stem just beneath the paper pot.

After a period of a month, the paper pot will be full of
roots, and at this stage the newly rooted plant can be severed
entirely from the old stem and replanted into a larger pot.
The bare stem will then break and produce new shoots

which will help to improve the appearance of the old plant.

The other plant of special interest is the arum lily, but in this case a rather special variety. Whilst visiting Warwick Castle gardens in 1938 I came across a dwarf arum lily which was also sweet scented. This was something entirely new to me, and I was able to procure a small plant which I later grew on to flowering size.

During the difficult war years I lost the majority of my arum stock, although I was able to save a few small growths. One of these when eventually grown on to flowering size proved to be even smaller than its predecessors. The reason for this was not apparent, but subsequently all the divisions taken from this plant retained this very dwarf habit.

The blooms are whiter than those of the ordinary arum lily, and they possess a delightful scent similar to that of a freesia. I exhibited this plant in May 1959 and it was duly recorded by the Royal Horticultural Society as *Zantedeschia aethiopica*, Aynhoe Park strain.

Of all my gardening associates to whom I have mentioned the dwarf sweet-scented arum, only one of them has known a similar plant. In fact I received a further two plants from this source, and once again they came from the Midlands. They were however approximately nine inches taller than the Aynhoe Park strain but they bore the same sweet scent, and in fact they were very similar to the plant I originally received from Warwick Castle gardens. There is no doubt that the exchange of plants between growers adds to the pleasure of gardening at all levels. Certainly, gardening has brought me in touch with an exceptionally wide field of people in all stations of life both near and from afar, which had it not been for my calling I would never have known. If the reader will bear with me I should like to recall some of these acquaintances, and relate how they came about.

One Sunday, I travelled with some gardening friends to Wylde Court near Newbury, the home of Sir William Cooke the famous orchid grower, to meet Mr. Rushton the chief grower. Whilst walking through the large cymbidium house, I noticed an old gentleman working amongst the plants. The old gentleman was in fact Sir William Cooke himself, and I was introduced to him by Mr. Rushton, who informed him that I was the grower of the cattleyas at Aynhoe Park. Sir William was at that time experimenting with raising and growing peaches in the open. As I had exhibited some peaches and nectarines at the R.H.S. a few weeks previously we had a great deal in common to discuss, and I spent a very informative couple of hours with Sir William, and at the end of that time he very kindly lent me some most useful gardening books.

On another more recent occasion, after I had completed the floral decorations for a party held by Mr. & Mrs. Hoare at South Street, London, I was invited to remain for the celebrations as I was informed that some of the guests would like to meet me. I was a little alarmed at this suggestion and felt sure that I would become an embarrassment at such a fashionable gathering. However, my fears were soon dispelled and the guests I met were both charming and natural and showed a genuine interest in gardening matters. Amongst them was Mr. Edmund de Rothschild, a keen orchid grower in his own right, and we had much to talk over, discussing the merits of various orchid plants. He also congratulated me on being awarded the R.H.S. long service medal a few weeks previously, and I was most pleasantly surprised that he should be aware of such mundane things.

I also met and had a most interesting discussion with Mary, Duchess of Roxburghe, who has a very lively interest in gardening, and finally I was able to renew an old acquaintance with Mrs. Hoare's mother, Viscountess Weir, with whom I immediately felt at ease for I have always found her to be a most gracious lady, and so a most eventful evening came to a satisfactory conclusion, and I was left with the thought that the seemingly wide gulfs in society are not really so wide after all.

Finally, to illustrate how a common interest can unite people across the face of the earth, I would like to tell you about a gardening friend of mine from Malaya, whom I have never met. A few weeks after I had published an article on the *Cattleya portia* in the *Amateur Gardening Journal*, I received a letter from the editor, Mr. Hellyer, informing me that a gentleman in Malaya, having read my article, wished to purchase a small plant or back growth of *Cattleya portia*. Could I help. I replied by saying I would be pleased to let their reader in Malaya have a small plant. A few weeks later I received the following letter from Malaya.

Dear Mr. Humphris,

I have just heard from Mr. Hellyer, who has gone way out of the usual track to be of assistance to an orchid lover half a world away, that you would be willing to let me have a small plant from your world-famous Portia. I am at a loss to find words to thank you for your offer.

All I can say is that your kindness and generosity has restored my tottering faith in humanity. Once again please accept my profound gratitude.

Yours faithfully,
Chow Ewe Boon.

Since receiving this letter we have corresponded regularly, but it was some months before I became aware through a friend of Mr. Boon's in London, that he was in fact Chinese. In one of my communications to Mr. Boon I requested him to write his next letter in Chinese as well as English. In his reply he wrote *I am afraid there is no room to write this letter in Chinese. I shall merely say in Chinese that I thank you very much for all the plants you have sent me, but then in classical Chinese, this simple statement is clothed in the most elaborate and ornate garb.* Below this was a beautiful design of Chinese letters.

CHAPTER TWENTY-ONE

Another Garden to Care for

IN 1960 MR. & MRS. HOARE ACQUIRED THE MAIN
part of another historic house in Buckinghamshire,
which, like the house of the Cartwright family at Aynhoe,
is no longer lived in by the family who originally built it.

Miss Elizabeth Cartwright also took up residence there
and made the nucleus of the Aynhoe Park treasures available to decorate the rooms there. The floral decorations and
pot plants were naturally provided from the Aynhoe greenhouses, thus keeping up the traditions of the past.

The task of designing a suitable garden was allocated to
Miss Brenda Colvin P.P.I.L.A., and it soon became obvious
to her that the basic problem was to adjust a small limited
area around the house to a new use.

The former layout was designed for a single owner
possessing the whole park with no intrusion from near
neighbours. The broad simple treatment, with the lawn
sweeping up to the house, unbroken by flower beds or other

incidents, and set in a well timbered park, was typical of the
18th-century landscape. Later additions in the form
of badly proportioned and insignificant rose beds and paths
could have been ignored and the original conception easily
restored, had the conditions of ownership been as they were
when the house was built. Now however, the house was to
be divided into flats, the main parts of the house on the
south and west side being occupied by Mr. & Mrs. Hoare
and Miss Cartwright, with an area of garden around them
allotted to their exclusive use.

Miss Colvin was asked to do for this garden what Sir
Charles Barry in the 19th century, and for different reasons,
had done for many others of its period.

An enclosure, dog-proof and child-proof, was essential. It
was decided that a low plastic mesh wire fence could be
hidden by box plants on either side to form a low wide evergreen hedge. Inside that a formal and symmetrical arrangement of beds and borders, planted with flowering shrubs,
perennials and annual plants to give a long lasting effect of
flowers and foliage, covering all seasons, would meet the
need of a personal garden with varied horticultural interests.
A paved terrace at the south east corner with a small border
and a yew hedge planted around three sides provided seclu-
sion for sitting out in spite of the lowness of the outer
hedge.

The former rose beds were to be sown down to grass so
as to match the surrounding lawn. This in itself was a
herculean task and one hundred and fifty tons of soil were
used before sowing, half of which was done in the autumn
of 1962, and the remainder in the spring of 1963. From this
time on all plants required for the garden and the house
were transported over forty miles from Aynhoe.

Mr. Hoare was extremely fond of liliums so I began to
grow liliums in pots again. This immediately took my mind
back to my apprentice days, especially with *Lilium auratum*,
also known as the Golden Lily of Japan. At Aynhoe *Lilium
auratum* held a special point of interest because Mr. Brown
as a young man worked at Veitchs' nursery. He told me the

first *auratum* to be seen in London was in·1862. The gardener in charge of the plant carried it from Veitchs' nursery to the Conservatory near the Albert Hall where the shows were held in those days, seated in a high dog cart with the precious plant held firmly between his knees.

Other liliums we grew were *Lilium regale*, sometimes called the Royal lily, *Lilium speciosum* var. *roseum* and *Lilium speciosum* var. *rubrum*.

Liliums can be grown successfully in an unheated greenhouse, and being protected from wind and rain, the flowers are produced in a state of perfect beauty. If the flowers are used for cutting, do not take more of the stem than is absolutely necessary, as the more stem left the better the new bulb will be. When the foliage has died down, store for the winter in a cool frost-proof shed or cupboard. In early spring they should be either re-potted or top dressed with fresh compost.

We found that a little dried cow manure placed on top of the crocks in the pot is very beneficial. When the bulbs are well rooted care must be exercised in watering because if they once get dry serious damage results.

Before going on holiday in June 1962 Mr. Hoare and I discussed several improvements in the garden, but on returning from my holiday I was shocked to receive a message from Mrs. Hoare to tell me that Mr. Hoare had peacefully passed away the previous day. So death once again robbed me of a kind and considerate employer, one who gave me every encouragement in my work, especially with the orchids. Mr. Hoare was also partly responsible for repairing and keeping the greenhouses at Aynhoe.

CHAPTER TWENTY-TWO

More TV Appearances

I N AUGUST 1960 I WAS INVITED BY THE B.B.C. TO
join Cliff Lewis on the *Gardening Club* stand at the
Radio and Television Show at Earls Court. The stand
consisted of a small greenhouse, and a small garden incorporating a lily pond and a variety of shrubs and plants.
I took a number of interesting plants with me from Aynhoe
which I displayed in the greenhouse. It turned out to be an
intriguing day and also an exhausting one, for we were in-
undated with queries from visitors to the show throughout
the day. Also it was a great pleasure and an education to
work alongside Cliff Lewis, and listen to the casual and
knowledgeable replies to the many and varied questions
asked of him.

So many people showed interest in the stand and came to
seek advice that we were obliged to recruit the services of
my son John, who had travelled to the show with me.
Although he is not a professional gardener, in fact he is in

the Police Force, he was able to answer many of the questions, and as a result our task was eased a little.

In January 1961 I made my second appearance on television in the programme *Gardening Club* and on this occasion I grasped the opportunity of getting a better insight into the enormous amount of work that goes into the production of a television programme.

The television studio floor covers an area of four thousand five hundred square feet. On arrival at the studio in the morning one is likely to find scene shifters removing the impedimenta used in the filming of a play or variety show. Once the materials which are no longer required have been removed, the same scene hands commence to erect the two greenhouses and lean-to shed used in the *Gardening Club* programme. This equipment is so constructed that it folds up like a pack of cards, and it can be assembled or dismantled in less than half an hour. There is of course no glass in the greenhouse, thus avoiding lamp reflection and enabling the camera lenses to move in really close on to its subject.

A heap of soil is also on hand, and often over a ton of earth is needed to construct a bed according to the needs of the particular programme. Normally such beds are about nine inches deep and are held into place on the studio floor by a surround of rocks. Finally a wattle fence is erected and beyond it a specially designed back cloth. A few paint marks on the floor represent crazy paving. Occasionally additional props are required. For example, Westmorland and York stone is on hand in case a wall or rockery is needed.

Once the set was completed I was able to stage the plants I had taken with me in the greenhouse. When this is completed, Paul Morby the producer and the lighting engineer discuss how best to light up the plants to show them to their best effect in order that they can be fully appreciated by the viewers. There is far more to *Gardening Club* than the dissemination of information and cultural advice. True garden lovers enjoy beauty or otherwise they would not labour patiently, and sometimes wait years to reap the rewards of their labour, and therefore this important aspect of their hobby is not forgotten, and it is not uncommon for the producer to spend as much as half an hour experimenting with camera positions, different lenses and shades of lighting in order to achieve the right effect.

In this particular programme I used polythene for the first time and illustrated to the viewers its great value in the greenhouse by partly lining the inside of the greenhouse which was put at my disposal.

To-day, polythene is an essential part of the gardener's equipment. It is manufactured by subjecting gas-ethylene, a substance derived from crude oil, to a very high temperature. It was discovered in 1933, and was converted into sheet film in 1938. The advantages of implementing double glazing in greenhouses in order to reduce loss of heat has long been appreciated, but the expense involved has prevented its general use. Polythene is the ideal substitute and where a glasshouse is fully lined with thick gauge polythene, it is almost as efficient as double glazing. However, in a house completely lined, and where there is no ventilation, moisture tends to condense rapidly on the lower side of the polythene, and therefore I find it more practical to affix the polythene inside the lower half of the roof only, leaving the ventilators uncovered. The walls can of course be completely lined.

It is of the utmost importance that the polythene be fixed tautly, so as to produce a smooth even surface, otherwise the smallest wrinkle will collect moisture which will form into globules and drip on to the plants below. Of course, a steep roof has a decided advantage in this respect and will lessen considerably the likelihood of drips, and therefore the polythene can be taken to a higher point than in the case of a shallow roof.

One thing to be borne in mind before deciding to use polythene is that although temperature is considerably increased, a slight loss of light will be experienced. However, less watering will be required, and in the majority of cases the advantages outweigh the disadvantages.

In June 1961, I received another invitation from Paul Morby to appear on *Gardening Club*. This time the programme was tele-recorded on Friday for transmission on the following Sunday afternoon. I welcomed this arrangement as it gave me the opportunity of seeing the programme for myself. After Percy Thrower introduced the programme, the first ten minutes consisted of film showing Percy dealing with problems in the vegetable garden. At the conclusion of the film he joined me in the greenhouse, and we discussed the merits of the plants which I had bought with me and which included orchids, gardenia, stephanotis, impatiens, pelargoniums, columnea, and sanseviera, and also a spike of *Strelitzia regina*, upon which the cameras were focused as the programme ended.

On this particular programme of *Gardening Club*, a live audience was present, made up of a party from the Institute of Public Relations who were visiting the studios on that day, and who had expressed a particular wish to watch *Gardening Club*. At the conclusion of the programme my wife and I were invited to meet the visitors, who were being entertained at a cocktail party given by the programme controller.

Both the gardenia and the *Strelitzia regina* were very much admired and I was required to answer numerous questions regarding their origin and cultivation.

The gardenia is an evergreen stove flowering shrub, and it was known in China more than two hundred years ago. It is very fragrant and was at one time a popular buttonhole flower. I keep my plant in the orchid house where the average winter temperature is 65 degrees Fahrenheit.

During the growing season, the atmosphere must be warm and moist, and the plant should be syringed frequently. It requires a compost consisting of one part fibrous loam, one part peat, and one part well-decayed manure, with a little charcoal and coarse silver sand added. It requires only moderate amounts of water from October to February, after which it should be watered freely, and when the pot becomes full of roots the plant should be fed regularly every seven to ten days. The gardenia is easily propagated by taking cuttings of firm young side shoots.

Strelitzia regina, or as it is commonly known, the Bird of Paradise flower, is one of the most exotic of all tropical plants. When seen in flower the reason for its intriguing nickname soon becomes apparent. The spikes which bear the blooms have a graceful bird-like head arching away from the stem with the blooms on either side unfolding like wings of a brilliant blue and orange hue.

The plant was first introduced into this country during the middle of the eighteenth century. Overseas visitors to Aynhoe Park have told me that they have seen masses of these Bird of Paradise plants growing wild in Tanzania.

Strelitzia regina is fairly easy to cultivate. It requires a warm house and can be planted either in a large pot or box, or alternatively it can be planted out, although it gives the best results when potted. The plants should be parted in early spring, and re-potted, using a compost of good fibrous loam, peat and a little charcoal. A liberal dressing of coarse bonemeal should also be added. They are gross feeders, and require occasional applications of Sequestrene to overcome iron deficiency.

The plants require very little water during winter months, but during summer they should be watered freely. It is a routine matter to raise strelitzia from seed, although this method means that it will be several years before the flowering stage is reached. The usual form of propagation therefore is by division.

The Bird of Paradise flower is so striking in its appearance that it is small wonder that it is becoming increasingly popular in floral arrangements in this country.

In August 1962 I had the pleasure of working with John Warren of Lincoln when I took part in a tele-recording for *Gardening Club*, entitled 'The uses and abuses of a Greenhouse'. Again I had the opportunity of displaying some of the more interesting varieties of greenhouse plants from the Aynhoe collection, including a bowl of stephanotis and *Boya carnosa* blooms.

Also included in this programme was a fine specimen of lemon, *Citrus ponderosa*. I first grew this most interesting plant from a rooted cutting which was sent to me from Scotland. The plant had an unusual history, for it had been rooted from a cutting which was part of a corsage brought from Florida, U.S.A.

Another plant which created great interest was the South African violet *Saintpaulia*. I am particularly fond of this enchanting little plant, and I recall reading an account in a gardening journal where its qualities were praised thus: '*Saintpaulia* is a violet, is a flower, is a joy.' It has deservedly become a very popular house plant. It is so popular in the States that in the late 1940's an American African Violet Society was formed, publishing a quarterly magazine.

The African violet was discovered in Tanzania by Walter van St. Paul, after whom it was named. It is easy to propagate, either from divisions, leaf cuttings or from seed sown in peat.

When rooting a plant, a short stem should be cut and immersed in a jar of water. Polythene placed over the neck of the container, with a small hole pierced in the centre for the stem to be pushed through, ensures that the leaves are kept above the water level. When the stem has rooted it should be transplanted into a small pot using a mixture of fibrous loam, peat and sand in equal parts. To ensure the successful cultivation of the violet, the water temperature of the plants should never be lower than the leaf temperature. It is important to remember that cold water causes blemishes to appear on the leaves, and will eventually kill the roots.

To ensure a healthy plant producing an abundance of flowers, the plant should be fed regularly once a week with plant food in a liquid form. *Saintpaulia*, being a native of Africa, is needless to say happier in warm temperatures, and will thrive in a temperature of 70 degrees Fahrenheit. In temperatures below 50 degrees Fahrenheit the leaves will tend to become spotted, and below 40 degrees Fahrenheit the plants will die. Light intensity forms a major part in bud formation. Too high a light intensity will scorch the leaves or harden their texture. The buds will form, but the flowers will rarely develop satisfactorily. However, if the light intensity is insufficient, the plant will form too much foliage, with the result that the flowers will be very scarce. It is therefore apparent that the ideal home for the plant is somewhere which is shaded from direct sunlight but which nevertheless affords the maximum amount of indirect light.

Beautiful plants can only be grown if clean healthy conditions are maintained. They appreciate a warm syringe about twice a week during the growing period, but it is imperative that the pot should not be left standing in water day after day, as the roots must have a circulation of air. Care must therefore be exercised to ensure that all excess water drains away, thus encouraging root creation. As one grower so aptly put it, 'They are temperamental little devils', but exceedingly exciting and rewarding when one has learned the knack of growing them.

During this television programme, I demonstrated a method I use of sowing small seed, such as begonia, and readers may also find this method of some practical use to them. First empty the seed from the packet into the left hand, ensuring prior to doing this that the palm of the hand is perfectly dry, otherwise the small fine seed will adhere to the skin. Tilt the palm slightly downwards, and then with your free hand gently tap the left wrist, at the same time passing the hand containing the seed backwards and forwards over the seed bed. After a little practice it will be found that it is possible to count each seed as it drops from the palm. To perfect this method of sowing it is a good idea to practice with a small amount of castor sugar.

In December 1963, Paul Morby again invited me to join Percy Thrower and John Warren in a programme to be televised from the new *Gardening Club* garden at Edgbaston. This consisted of a plot of land measuring one hundred and forty feet by thirty feet, adjoining the Botanical Gardens. It had been well-used as a typical family weekend retreat, and was a tribute to Mr. Fred Saunders who was in charge of its cultivation. At this time an Oakworth greenhouse was erected there. It was of tubular construction, measuring fifteen feet by eleven feet. Its electric heating system was thermostatically controlled, and in addition it was installed with a propagating unit complete with soil-warming tables. Without the usual studio facilities a number of problems were encountered in presenting the programme. The camera had to be placed in the doorway of the greenhouse, and a number of panes of glass needed to be removed for close-up shots, and of course the problem causing the most concern was completely out of our hands, namely the weather.

On the actual day our worst fears were confirmed, and the elements conspired to upset the carefully planned arrangements. John Warren was prevented from appearing because of dense fog on the roads, although fortunately it was not very dense at Edgbaston itself. However, it was extremely cold and the light was far from good, and consequently the programme went through almost unrehearsed.

After discussing the general condition of the garden, and some shrubs which had stood the winter, Percy Thrower joined me in the greenhouse, where I had a small collection of plants, including some orchids which were growing under a small polythene tent which had been erected at the warm end of the greenhouse. Whilst discussing a miniature cymbidium, the cameraman found that part of his camera had become wedged beneath the eaves of the greenhouse, and thus he was able to focus only on the lower half of the plant. Percy immediately noticed his predicament after glancing at the monitor, and very quickly he leaned forward and tilted the plant so that it appeared in its entirety on the screen, whilst I was discussing it without any noticeable break in the continuity. I have always been impressed by this kind of team spirit which ensures that television programmes always appear to run smoothly.

Amongst the orchids portrayed in this programme was a small plant of *Cypripedium niveum*. This was one of several small plants despatched to me from Pulase Larigauri by Mr. Boon in 1962. There was also some *Cypripedium barbatum* from the Penang Hills, and some spathoglottis. Mr. Boon has also told me of a cymbidium which grows wild in the Penang area, and which bears pendulous maroon flowers on stems three feet in length, and he described a very fine species of *arachnis*, the spider orchid. On reading such glowing accounts of these luxurious plants growing in their natural conditions, one is apt to become envious of those who live in such surroundings, although the picture conjured up by the mind may be sometimes exaggerated. Whilst *Cypripedium niveum* used at one time to abound in and around Penang, the natural supply has now become very depleted, mainly because American fanciers have bought up the plants, sometimes paying very high prices for them. Nowadays if one requires native plants it becomes necessary to go on safari into the jungle. As Mr. Boon explains, one does not venture into the Malayan jungle alone.

In May 1965, I gained another certificate of Cultural Commendation for a large specimen plant of *Cattleya skinneri*. This is a beautiful specimen which originally came from Guatemala. This particular plant was in 1960 growing in a native cottage just outside Barbados, and was sent to me by air. It arrived in a very dry shrivelled condition and took nearly two years to recover.

Another showy flower I like is *Odontoglossum grande*, sometimes referred to as tiger orchid, but chiefly as the clown orchid, so called on account of a delightful mimicry of a clown in the centre of the flower. The spreading flowers, five to six inches in diameter, are yellow, heavily barred with chestnut brown, with a bright varnished finish. They also make good cut flowers.

On a well grown plant the leaves are tough and leathery, the pseudo bulbs stout and hard so that the plant will tolerate a variety of conditions. Temperature during the winter should be around 50 degrees Fahrenheit with corresponding higher temperatures during the summer. While resting, only give the plant sufficient water to keep the pseudo bulbs from shrivelling. At the time of writing I have a plant carrying eight spikes with forty-seven blooms. One bulb has two spikes, one with eight blooms, the other with five.

Whilst writing these last chapters I have once more had the pleasure of appearing in the B.B.C. *Gardening Club* programme with Percy Thrower.

On this occasion I demonstrated to viewers the method I employ when dividing and re-potting cymbidiums. During the programme I explained that it was possible to utilise substitutes for osmunda fibre, which was becoming increasingly expensive. The compost I used consisted of coarse peat, good fibrous loam with the soil teased out, using only the root fibre, and oak or beech leaves (not leaf soil). The leaves should be partly decayed and cut into half to one inch squares before use. The stems and leaf stalks of bracken similarly cut can also be used. With this mixture it is necessary only to use one part osmunda fibre and one part sphagnum moss as a top dressing.

I understand that Mr. F. Griffen of the Central Orchid Society, Wolverhampton, has successfully used pine needles as a substitute for osmunda fibre. If this method is employed it is important that the needles should be clean and dry when gathered, and if they are soaked in warm water before use they are easier to handle.

Quite often orchid growers become disappointed when their cymbidiums do not flower as well as expected, perhaps producing a flower spike only bi-annually. The reason for their failure is of course due to cultural errors, and therefore the utmost care should be taken when re-potting.

During the television programme I exhibited a seedling *Cymbidium pauwelsii* Compte de Hemptine *F.C.C.* x *Alexanderii westonbirt F.C.C.*, which is about seven years old. Two years previously it produced a spike of six blooms on the third bulb and also a young growth appeared. The following year the plant produced two spikes each with seven blooms, and this year to my amazement a further two spikes each with seven blooms appeared on the same bulb. This was the first time that I had either seen or heard of a plant producing four spikes from one bulb. It was most rewarding and made all the preparation and care that had gone into the cultivation of the plant worthwhile.

Conclusion

DURING MY FIFTY-FIRST YEAR AT AYNHOE PARK yet another dramatic change has taken place in the domestic situation of the Cartwright family. Miss Elizabeth Cartwright, the only direct surviving member of the family, has purchased a house and taken up residence in the west country where she has some family connections through her late grandmother.

I shall now have the task of building up a collection from the plants at Aynhoe for the new home and so start a new chapter in a long and varied career in horticulture.

Miss Cartwright's new home is a magnificent stone-built house, mainly of Elizabethan and classical 18th-century construction. The gardens cover eighteen acres, mostly wooded glades and some agricultural land. One very pleasing feature is an old mill which is being restored.

The house was sold on condition that the new owner continued to maintain the garden and the ornamental treasures in it. These treasures, which span two thousand years from Greek 3rd century B.C. to Italian Renaissance, were collected by a former owner from the continent before the days when exports of national treasures were forbidden.

Many of the rare treasures at present at Aynhoe will eventually be transported there and will enhance the beauty of the new home. Amongst these treasures there is one that I am particularly fond of. It is a bible which was published in 1672, one of the Cartwright family's most precious heirlooms. This most rare and valuable book is illustrated with many beautiful hand-painted pictures, two of which appeal to me as a gardener. One is of Adam and Eve being driven from the Garden of Eden, and the other depicts the Resurrection and portrays Mary Magdalen kneeling at the empty tomb and looking across to the figure of Christ whom she mistook for the gardener.

Possibly one day in the future I may be able to help convey the large *Cattleya portia* to the west country and thus add to the natural beauty of the house. I have already discussed with my assistant how best this mammoth task might be accomplished.

In November 1967, Lady Cartwright died, and whilst helping to line the grave, I glanced at a head stone a few feet away and recalled that fifty-two years before, I had helped line the grave for William Cornwallis Cartwright. The thought also came to my mind that during that time I had assisted in the burial of four generations of the Cartwright family. With the passing of Lady Cartwright, for the first time in over three hundred and fifty years there is no longer a member of the family residing in Aynhoe.

At the time of this book going to print, I am still gardening on at Aynhoe Park, albeit a very small part of the Aynhoe Park I knew when I started work there as a boy over fifty years ago, for most of the gardens and the beautiful surrounding park land have now passed from the Cartwright family and much of it has recently been developed. Modern housing estates have mushroomed where once there were orchards, rose gardens and flower-filled greenhouses.

I mourn its passing, but I shall remain forever thankful that I have known its most glorious years, and have shared in the countless pleasures which only a gardener can experience. *One is nearer to God in the garden, than anywhere else on the earth.* This is a well worn saying, but nevertheless a very true one, and I shall have many wonderful memories to savour during the years ahead.

Soon I may have to retire, but I shall do so reluctantly, for there are so many new horizons and avenues yet to be explored in the world of horticulture. Time marches relentlessly on however, and my young assistant at Aynhoe will undoubtedly experience the same excitement, sense of achievement and satisfaction amongst his plants, that I and all other life-time gardeners have known.

In this synthetic 20th-century age in which we now live, where the strain and tempo of everyday life inevitably take their toll on us all, it is still possible to find peace of mind and to escape the pressures of modern life in the garden or in the greenhouse, and I shall feel that this book has been worthwhile if it has helped to transport the reader away from these cares for a short while, and perhaps has also given encouragement to a number of prospective young gardeners.

I fervently hope that this record has afforded all my gardening friends some interesting reading, and also that they have found some of the material contained herein of some practical use.

Index

213